Killer

CW01507719

The Horrifying Story of Serial Killer John Wayne Gacy (True Crime)

By

James Richmond

within this book has been derived from various sources. Please consult a licensed professional before attempting any techniques outlined in this book.

By reading this document, the reader agrees that under no circumstances is the author responsible for any losses, direct or indirect, that are incurred as a result of the use of information contained within this document, including, but not limited to, errors, omissions, or inaccuracies.

CONTENTS

Introduction

Rows of houses decorated with bright, flashing lights slept in the still night. Kind neighbors prepared for the holidays quickly approaching. In two days, children would leap from under their covers and storm into their parents' bedroom, asking if Santa visited. It was only a couple of days from Christmas when the corpses of two young men were uncovered— pulled from a crawl space in the sleepy Chicago suburbs. At that time, December 23, 1978, during the bitter winter night, one of the most horrifying excavations began.

While many homes prepared to celebrate Christmas, the families on Summerdale watched in horror as the police tore through the crawl space of John Wayne Gacy's two-bedroom ranch. Buckets of cement and soil were pulled to the surface. Body after body emerged, and with them, the jarring truth. Their kind and gregarious neighbor was one of the deadliest serial killers in American history.

Through the passage hidden in the bedroom, the police descended. At first, the horrible methane gas halted the initial investigation. The process of putrefaction was in full force, smothering the crawl space with noxious gases inciting nausea and dizziness. Some of the corpses had been rotting beneath the floorboards for years. Built on swampland, the crawl space's constant flooding created the adipocere's gray waxy substance to form on the soft tissue and create an intolerable scent. The water mixed with the layers of lime spread by Gacy in an attempt to hasten decomposition and rid his home of the putrid odor, seeping into the graves, dissolving the bodies into a murderous soup.

Investigators wore jumpsuits and charcoal filtered masks to protect them as they dove into the grizzly crime scene. Their work would take weeks, weeks of a grueling process, fighting through the hellish space. They removed the floorboards to alleviate some of the gases and add light. The fresher bodies bloated, filling with gases and bacteria. The skin had transformed into a greenish-black hue, signifying active decomposition. Damaged blood cells and liquified tissues leaked from the bodies setting into the soil. Others, beneath slabs of concrete, were nothing more than bone and gray skin clinging together. Some of the bodies were discovered with underwear jammed into their throats, others in plastic bags or with ropes around their necks.

The police used an intricate map drawn by John Wayne Gacy after his arrest to uncover the tomb. The bodies were meticulously aligned, some paired with others.

Many of Gacy's victims were members of society who were forgotten or looked down upon. Criminologist Steven A. Egger referred to them as the "less dead." Sex workers, gay people, and young adults who had run away from home fell into this category. And many criminals took advantage of them, especially Gacy. Gacy paraded through the night under the guise of an undercover cop and would hire sex workers to mutilate. He found them at the bus station or lured young employees to his home.

It took five reports against Gacy before he was seriously investigated by the police.

When all twenty-nine bodies were removed from the property and four more found off the bank of the Des Plaines River, 8213 Summerdale became nothing more than a haunting landmark of John Wayne Gacy's murderous rampage.

The media and onlookers swarmed the neighborhood to look upon the brick ranch with Christmas lights ominously blinking. They wanted to understand who John Wayne Gacy was. How could the neighbors be unaware of the murders taking place behind the curtains, with only a few feet of green lawn separating them?

John Wayne Gacy's charm fooled the next-door families. He was a master manipulator and a well-known figure in the community, but with a terrible secret. From 1972 until 1978, he lured thirty-three innocent teenagers and young men to their unsuspecting deaths. His crimes were violent and torturous, but to those who knew him personally, he was a smart and gregarious businessman on the rise of the Chicago political scene, who volunteered to dress up as a clown and help sick children smile. Gacy had fooled almost everyone.

He hosted elaborate parties, inviting hundreds over to his home. The same house where lifeless bodies lay still beneath the floorboards, forever silent. And when guests asked about the strange scent, he told them it was nothing more than dampness in the crawl space. Few had reason to doubt him, to suspect that Gacy was capable of raping and strangling so many young men. Some of which were his very own employees, who unknowingly dug the graves for Gacy beneath the foundation under the guise of home improvement. He manipulated them, enticing them with offers of money or employment, and used various tricks to subdue them. Some even dug their very own graves. His favorite method of killing was to trap them with handcuffs.

After several rounds of drinks, Gacy asked victims if they wanted to learn how to break free from a pair of metal cuffs. Upon agreeing, Gacy slipped the cuffs onto their wrists. Imprisoned with no hope to escape. Next came the rope trick. He tied a noose around his victim's neck, creating a garrote to twist the rope and render his victim unconscious within ten to thirty seconds, then dead in as little as one minute.

In a perverted twist of irony, those same handcuffs were used as an innocent trick to entertain sick children when Gacy dressed fully as a clown. He donned the makeup, painting the red smile and blue eyes upon his face with sharp points, which contrasts the rounded welcoming shape of happy clowns. Pogo the Clown, as he was known, would handcuff himself and wiggle his way out by using a key kept hidden in his sleeve. Unlike his victims, who were never set free.

Dubbed the "killer clown" by the media, Gacy solidified the public's fear of evil clowns. With exaggerated features and unpredictable behavior, the clown has become the star of urban legends and horror stories. The fear of clowns even has its own name, "Coulrophobia," which translates to "a fear of someone who walks on stilts." For many, the fright stems from the unknown. The identity of the clown is hidden away, buried beneath the costume and white paint. The representation of clowns such as Stephen King's *It* and the terrifying clowns who chased down people in America during 2016 all helped propel the panic around clowns, but none compared to the real horror of John Wayne Gacy. For he represents the truth—a friendly neighbor can don a costume, entertain children at parties, and just as easily commit crimes far darker than any nightmare imaginable. The clown, a symbol of innocence and fun, could be a monster capable of rape and murder.

It is the fear of the person beneath it all. In John Wayne Gacy, something genuinely sinister and malicious was buried beneath the makeup. Something capable of pure evil.

But Gacy knew this.

He told the police before he was arrested and charged, "A clown can get away with murder."

A Father and His Son

It was St. Patrick's Day in Chicago; twenty-nine minutes after midnight on the cold spring night of March 17, 1942, Edgewater Hospital on the northside welcomed a brand-new baby boy into the world. The father was forty-one-year-old John Stanley Gacy, a Chicago native, American soldier, and machinist. He was a World War I veteran and married to Marion Elaine Robinson. They named their new bundle of joy, John Wayne Gacy, after the American film star. They hoped their son would embody the epitome of masculinity.

The parents left the hospital, and upon returning home, they introduced the baby to his sister, Joanne, who was only two years old. After another two years went by, the Polish family welcomed another baby, this time a girl named Karen.

John grew up in a safe neighborhood on Chicago's northside. His neighbors did not struggle for money. The houses on the block were well maintained with grand yards full of vegetable gardens and well-maintained flowers. Nearby railroads ran east and south toward the city.

For John Wayne Gacy, he remembered the bits of childhood with fondness. He recalled his first memory of taking the train to visit his aunt and uncle. Another time, he remembered walking out of the house into the front yard naked, too young to even care. Everyone laughed endearingly at the sight of young John's indecent exposure. Summer nights were spent running around outside catching fireflies or sneaking into neighbors' yards to be chased away.

But behind the veil of nostalgic memories, darkness loomed like a shadow. John Wayne Gacy was never enough for his father. An alcoholic who worked all day as an auto machinist and came home to drink before supper. The family waited and heard the heavy footsteps as John Stanley Gacy emerged from the basement, coming up the stairs. God forbid if any of the children misbehaved. Any sign of disobedience was met with a beating from the razor strop kept hanging on the wall. Its presence was a foreboding reminder to the three children. His father was not shy to hit his children with the makeshift whip, and his vile anger could switch on at any moment. The three children learned to toughen up against the wrath of their father—especially John, who would not cry as John Stanley beat him.

The children experienced plenty of abuse from their father, but Marion often took the brunt of her husband's aggression. The greatest danger was that the episodes of anger could be spontaneous or without any catalyst.

It was a warm summer night. John was only two years old, and the family sat around the dinner table for their supper. Marion was back home with a three-week-old Karen. "I don't know what triggered it," she said. Without any reason, John Stanley became blinded with a violent fit of rage. He whipped a plate of food at

Marion. Then he rose from the table and struck her face with enough force to knock the bridge of her teeth out. Screams erupted from the three young children who watched in horror. Blood gushed from Marion's face as she ran out of the house into the night. Her husband chased after her. During the chaos, a neighbor rushed out to defend Marion and shouted out, "Don't hit her again! I'm calling the police!"

With his gun in hand, John Stanley stormed out of the house and disappeared for several days. Marion gathered the children and left to stay at her brother's. After several days, Marion finally made the decision to return home. The plate of food remained stuck to the wall where her husband had thrown it. She cleaned the mess that she did not create and prepared her husband's favorite dinner—boiled meat and potatoes. When he returned, they ate dinner and carried on as though John Stanley had not attacked his wife only a few days prior.

Marion sought ways to explain her husband's violence. She blamed his blow-ups on a benign brain tumor even though the doctors told her it did not affect his temper. It was a rationalization she used for the rest of her life to explain John Stanley's erratic behavior. She thought when he started drinking, his brain would swell up, and the tumor created pressure. He couldn't help it.

The abuse John Stanley gave was not limited to random outbursts. He berated his son constantly and called him a sissy. It began when he was only four years old. John was out in the garage with his father, who was working on the car. He was only a small child and managed to scramble a pile of car parts on the floor. John Stanley erupted into a fit of anger and beat his son, spewing lines of insults. A flood of violence poured forth all because of a few pieces of metal shifting position.

It was clear early on that John was unlike the other boys. He was a bit strange and a loner. Born with an enlarged bottleneck heart, John couldn't participate in sports with the other neighborhood boys. He was sickly, weak, and overweight, even at a young age—

all more reason for his father to look down upon him. John Stanley's only son was soft.

Hidden from his father's spiteful eye, the young John spent his time hiding underneath the front porch where his father built a sandbox for him. There he spent his time. While other boys played sports and raced around outside, John remained tucked away from the rest of the world, letting his imagination take over.

According to Gacy, it was at this young age he experienced his first sexual assault. An older girl from the neighborhood on Opal Street coerced him away from his home to a prairie hidden away from the watchful adult eyes. There in the tall grass, she took advantage of the little boy. Not knowing any better, young John lay helpless as the older girl fondled him. When he told his parents, they began to shout and fight with one another.

Only three years later, it was 1949. John, seven at the time, was with another neighborhood boy and the boy's younger sister. It all may have started as innocent playing, but the playing progressed until it became unsettling. All the children became naked. John recalled how he and the boy messed around sexually with the younger sister. When his father found out, he was beaten with the razor strop.

Around the same time, John Stanley had a contractor friend who took a liking to Gacy. The family friend invited Gacy along in his truck for rides to construction sites. For a seven-year-old Gacy, these drives were terrible. He dreaded them. While he enjoyed building and construction, his father's friend would wrestle with Gacy. The playful roughhousing usually ended with Gacy's head pinned in the man's crotch, his face pressed against the men's rugged work jeans. John Stanley's friend was messing around with Gacy the same way Gacy had with the little girl. But Gacy felt personal shame about what the contractor did and never spoke about the strange wrestling matches. He feared his father would become angry and think he was a "jag off" or a "fruit picker." There was nothing more John Stanley hated than gay people.

At home, John's behavior may have clued his parents off to the concerning and peculiar sexual experiences he was exposed to in his early childhood. While Gacy was still around seven or eight, John Stanley and his wife Marion were getting dressed to go out. Marion opened her underwear drawer to find every piece missing. The parents searched for the weird disappearance. The garments were not in their room nor the laundry. Eventually, they found them stashed away. Their son had stuffed it all in a brown bag and stuck it beneath the porch. He claimed he had no clue why the underwear was hidden away in his sandbox when questioned later. His parents continued to interrogate him until Gacy finally claimed that he liked the feel of it. Rather than address the obvious issues, John Stanley pulled the razor strop off the wall and began to beat his son.

The fetish with underwear surfaced when he was younger, but Gacy never stopped stealing his mother's underwear. Marion made a point never to mention it to her husband again. Perhaps she was trying to keep her son safe from his father's unforgiving rage. She saw how John Stanley treated her baby boy. She witnessed how her husband screamed and beat her child. Marion's maternal protection could have led John to become a mama's boy. He stayed close to her and loved her dearly. He was safe with her.

John's parents may have tried to counteract the strange behavior they saw in their child by enrolling him in Catholic school. Maybe in their eyes, a religious influence could help shape him into a moral, normal person. He attended the school with his sisters until the age of eleven. The Gacy's moved around this time, and so John Wayne Gacy began to attend public school. For the most part, he was a well-behaved student. He kept himself busy. In the mornings, he worked a newspaper route, and in the evenings, he had a part-time job at a grocery store.

The new house was larger and positioned closer to the Chicago proper. In the dark basement, John Stanley spent most of his time. To John, it was his father's sacred place. A place kept hidden with several locks. Only his father held the key. Hidden away in his downstairs cave, John Stanley drank and became angry. At times, the family heard shouting. It was John Stanley speaking to himself from the depths of the house.

As an outstanding rule, no one ate supper until he was ready. He would return to the surface accompanied by aggressive stomping up the stairs. Emerging from the basement, he was eager to argue with anyone. He'd holler at his young children, call them dumb and stupid. "If my father said the sun wouldn't rise tomorrow," John later described, "you couldn't disagree with him. He'd argue you into the ground. But when I was young, I didn't know. I argued with him, and he'd holler at me. Tell me I was dumb and stupid. Arguing with little kids, and every time he had to win. Never wrong."

To further the distance between father and son's relationship, John's health conditions restricted him from participating in any sports. "So I was a disappointment to my dad," John said, "because I was weak, and he was strong. He hated the weak person, even in emotions. We'd go to funerals for someone in the family, and he'd never get tears in his eyes. At a party, he'd never laugh—a strong, somber individual. Emotion was a weakness. Physical illness, even when it couldn't be helped, was a weakness. I remember once he was so sick, he couldn't get out of bed, and Ma finally called a doctor. The doctor said, 'How long have you been like this?' My dad said, 'Ten days.' The doctor said, 'Why didn't you wait another day and just call the undertaker?' And it turned out my dad had pneumonia."

John's father was a callous and cold individual to everyone in his family. His behavior created an uncertain environment for everyone in his home. His wife and children experienced the worst of his behavior and abuse. But Marion continued to insist it was the tumor's fault.

And the same year of the move, John went out to play on the swing. He must have lost control or was being a little too wild, as children do, and smacked his head hard on the metal pole. Hard enough to black out.

His body fell from the swing onto the ground. From that moment forward, John began to suffer from episodes of blacking out. Suddenly, he would pass out for ten minutes at a time. After many visits to doctors and hospitals, there was no clear answer. No explanation. But to John Stanley, his son was merely faking to get out of school. The child was too weak and used a simple head bump as an excuse to be lazy. That's all it ever was to John Stanley—a way for his son to get out of situations.

When John stopped attending the public grammar school where he was failing, he moved to a vocational school. There he surpassed the other students. He did so well in science that his teacher encouraged him to stop attending class and work. He ran errands for the teachers and did office work.

Among the staff and students, he gained a reputation for being well-dressed. His clothes weren't expensive, but the outfits were well thought out. He was neat and orderly. Even his sister's girlfriends noticed how tidy he was. They'd laugh and say he kept his room better than their own. He wasn't able to be a part of any sports with his classmates, but he was the Civil Defense captain in high school.

Usually, boys his age thought about companionship and meeting girls. Gacy did not share their enthusiasm to couple up. Instead of dating, he continued pursuing his work. He started his career in Chicago politics as an assistant precinct captain to the Democratic candidate for alderman in the 45th Ward.

His father disapproved. Politicians, to John Stanley, were scum and crooks. He called his son a fool, but John disagreed and continued "to work his ass off." John recalled, "Maybe it was a way to antagonize my dad. In part. And maybe it was a way to get acceptance. I was always looking for acceptance because my dad made me feel that I was never good enough."

John Stanley's approval for his son never came. The lack of support might have reinforced Gacy's habit of comparing himself to the other boys in his classes and age. They were muscular, athletic. John wasn't. As a teenager, he stood five feet eight inches and was nearing two hundred pounds. He was unhappy with how he viewed himself. It was around the age of sixteen when John dwelled on death often. His Catholic faith kept him from drifting to thoughts of suicide. Instead, he thought of dying as the darkest shadow, a faceless figure that arrived as the Lord's blessing. The dark contemplation resulted from different ways he felt inadequate.

He couldn't be a part of the football team with the other male students, but there was one sport John could safely participate in—bowling. He joined a group affiliated with the St. John Berchmans' parish Holy Name Society. He was decent at it. Bowling created opportunities for John to work within the parish. He began to toy with the idea of becoming a priest. It seemed to be the perfect fit. He could help people and gain a measure of respect. During his time, he organized a young adults group to keep young men within the Catholic church. He worked hard, repenting, and visited the confessional often.

Confession was a way for John to become clean again. It felt right. Sunday nights were spent playing cards with the parish priests. They spoke about John becoming one. It made sense. He was around the church often, found success in keeping young men within the faith. As they sat in the old church, the deck of cards moving within their hands, they encouraged him that perhaps God was speaking to him quite directly. John knew he liked helping people, and he also knew that celibacy would be no problem for him. Unlike his peers, he had no sex drive. He described himself at that age later in an interview, "I was sickly, and I certainly wasn't no physically built individual, and I didn't have no sex drive, so being a priest seemed perfect, a natural thing to do for a kid like me." For John back then, having a "broad" around was nothing more than a headache. He saw a wife as stupid and bothersome.

While John saw the priesthood as the perfect fit for his future, his father accusingly called him a queer. He saw it residing in his father's eyes, a look of disgust. As if his father knew that every time John came home late and blamed his tardiness on scoring with a girl, he was lying.

His father's icy stares of contempt and disbelief followed John.

But John Wayne Gacy figured he had only been a late bloomer when it came to sex.

In his car, parked somewhere private, he and some woman were necking. Nervously, his hands reached as he pulled off her blouse and then her skirt until she was naked right there in front of him. She was exposed to Gacy, waiting for his next move. He looked over her milky, soft skin, but he froze.

Marion was the one who taught John about sex. He remembered everything his mother had told him. It was something special between two people, and if he could satisfy his partner, he satisfied himself. That night, he liked the way his date looked and enjoyed the appearance of her body. But the process of it all felt forced as if it were some duty put upon him. Something happened then. Darkness came over, and John passed out, right then, as he had when he was a child all those times. And when he came to, his head hurt, and he found himself slumped forward in the seat. His date had already put her clothes back on.

He returned home to tell his father, who became angry when John admitted to passing out. To John Stanley, it had all been an act for attention. His son wasn't sick; he was afraid. The whole date, the almost intimacy, it was all fake, and his son was petrified of it.

John Wayne Gacy grew older. Even at the age of twenty, he was unable to finish high school. Tensions were higher than ever at home. It came down to a fight over a distributor cap with his father. That was the last straw. John decided to leave home. He took the car he still owed his father money for and headed out west. Alone for the first time, he ended up in Las Vegas working at Palm Mortuary. He began as a companion in the ambulance. Then they found out he was not yet twenty-one and had lied about his age. John was promptly demoted. He was forced to leave the exciting job of bright flashing lights and the ambulance to work in the dark, haunting mortuary.

He watched as the bodies came in and paid particular attention to the young men. They had strong muscular bodies, and they represented everything John was supposed to be but wasn't. Yet, they were the ones who found death first, not sickly, weak John. While John worked, he observed the morticians closely and the embalming process. It captivated him, and he watched until he thought he could do it himself. And when no one was around, John Wayne Gacy admitted to conducting what he called "experiments" on the corpses.

He recounted an evening in the dark of the mortuary basement, with all the lights off, he spotted an open coffin. Inside was the body of a young man. John climbed in beside the cold body to lay beside it in the silence. A fear came over as he pressed against the lifeless young man. A terrible fear. It scared him so severely that he phoned his mother the next day and asked if his father would let him return home.

Businessman in the Making

J ohn Wayne Gacy moved back home. There he was no longer a transient nobody like he was in Vegas. He wasn't alone anymore.

That time on his own taught John a few life lessons. Without a high school diploma, he managed to talk his way into admission to Northwestern Business College. He took year-long courses and graduated with success. Both his parents attended his graduation, posing for photos with their son. With a degree in hand, he snagged a job at Nunn-Bush Shoes and worked his way up to manager. He sold shoes like none other. John was a talker. He had a gregarious way and spoke with articulation. He was bred to sell. Everyone noticed the energy around him, the knack he had to pull people in. After observing his great sales success, he was transferred to one of the main department stores out in Springfield. For John, this was a huge promotion.

The promotion led him to move in with his aunt and uncle, finally away from the cold, harsh judgment of John Stanley. He was back on his feet and moving forward with his own life.

He began to date frequently. He joined the Springfield Junior Chamber of Commerce, a group known as the Jaycees. John went above and beyond for the Jaycees. He ran a Christmas parade with wild success.

His new love of life resulted in finding a partner. In September of 1964, John Wayne Gacy married Marlynn Myers, a pretty coworker. What John lacked in looks, he made up for with charm and confidence. She admired the way he sold shoes as well as how he sold himself. She watched the way he worked with customers and enjoyed talking with him. To Marlynn, John painted himself as a big spender who hailed from the city. He boasted about his life experience, even at such a young age. Her parents bought a string of Kentucky Fried Chickens and left their home to the newlyweds. Life was finally looking up for John Wayne Gacy.

And in the next year, he was named the Jaycees' first vice president. He was finally receiving the recognition among young business professionals he had so eagerly sought after. His young wife was pregnant, and he had, without a doubt, proved his old man very wrong.

It was a period that could be considered some of the best years for John. His family and sisters were doing well. John Stanley was finally beginning to speak to his son like a man. He was finally respected, and that was what he always desired.

It was also around this time he had his first sexual experience with a man. It was 1964, right before he was married. John was out with an older fellow. They grabbed a few drinks as friends when they decided they wanted to go out and pick up some girls. They did so without success, and with a robust alcoholic-induced buzz, their night was coming to a close. This was when Richard Stuart invited John over for some coffee.

John later described the night as he sat in Richard's home, drunk and young: "But instead, we had more drinks. Or I did. And Richard was telling me, he said, 'You know, you go out looking for women, you strike out, you probably go home and play with yourself. Me, I don't give a shit who blows me. A mouth is a mouth. So if I strike out with women, I pick up a guy. Which means on any given night, I got twice the chance to score than you do.'"

The darkness returned like it had that night with the date in his car. He passed out. And when he came to, he was naked, and Richard was performing oral on John. To John, he was too young and naive to know how to handle the situation. He realized it felt good, and so he didn't stop Richard. But afterward, he spun into a depression. To John, that was one of the lowest periods of his life.

Outside of his most recent sexual assault, Gacy's life was transforming. And his father-in-law's success with KFC was going well. He needed a new manager for one of his restaurants. And although Marlynn's father never liked his son-in-law that much, he wanted his only child close to him. He offered to pay for Gacy's house in Waterloo if he'd come work for the restaurant chain.

John dove into the work with gusto. His job kept him busy for ten to fourteen hours a day. Even with the demanding schedule, he managed to find time to join the Waterloo Junior Chamber of Commerce. He worked tirelessly well into the night on the Jaycees. He volunteered for projects and went above and beyond like no other member ever had. He was seen as a tireless worker but also as a braggart and overbearing. He insisted that his workers and fellow members would refer to him as the "colonel." But no matter how much John got on the other members' nerves, there was no denying how hard of a worker he was. When John found out the Jaycees were twenty-three members short of their quota, John went out that very day and personally recruited twenty new members. Running three of the KFCs, John was able to provide his club with free chicken for meals. This may have acted as a bit of a bargaining chip to earn other's approval.

A manipulative streak was seen in John. He moved with an air, similar to a con artist. He wasn't afraid to manipulate people. He would sometimes go to what others thought of as extreme to gain favor.

There was an evening at supper when John offered his wife Marlynn to the President of the Jaycees, Charles Hill. After dinner at Hill's home, and while the wives were in the kitchen, John asked Hill if he liked the dress Marlynn was wearing. Hill responded with a simple yes. But John pushed the matter further as the women were out of earshot.

"Do you like her?" he asked again. Hill agreed, saying he always had. Gacy was pleased by the answer and told Hill that Marlynn had always liked Hill as well. And then, in the evening, he leaned closer. "Do you want her?" John asked. Confusion came across Hill. He wasn't sure exactly how to respond to the offer. He simply reminded John that the two of them were friends. John laughed it off. It was only a joke. At least that was the only way Hill knew how to understand the exchange.

John's whole social world revolved around the Jaycees. He rose in the ranks and landed a spot on the board of directors in 1967. He even managed to coordinate and plan one of the most successful Jaycee events of the year. Even when the rumor spurred that some of the young Jaycee members were involved with wife swapping, no one pried. John had been named the best Jaycee club chaplain in all of Iowa that year. It was no one's business what he did behind doors.

His long days didn't stop there. John had joined a group called the Merchant Police. It was a group of ordinary civilians who took it upon themselves to supplement the police. For Gacy, it was an opportunity to establish more power. It was noted by the other members how much he enjoyed playing the role of a cop. It was strange to them. A red flashing light was stuck to the top of his car. He carried a gun for protection. Deterring crime, looking for suspicious activity gave him some sort of satisfaction. John's love for police work was no secret. He would take buckets of free chicken over to the station, even to his father-in-law's disapproval. It was a strategic move on his behalf. Gacy believed having the police on your side came with significant advantages.

He figured, if the cops liked him, they wouldn't arrest him. If he left the bar a little drunk and drove home, they'd send him on his way, ticket free. They wouldn't care if the Jaycees were throwing a stag party with prostitutes, and if some of the officers attended, they could never turn him in. Gacy wanted to be untouchable in Waterloo.

There on Fairlane Street, John and his wife lived in a bungalow. He was only twenty-six years old, and to everyone around him, he was living the perfect life. His wife had given birth to a son, and in '67, the young family welcomed a baby girl.

Even John Stanley came up from Chicago to visit his son. They drove around in Gacy's brand-new Olds Vista Cruiser and spoke like a real father and son might. A real conversation. There was no yelling, no fighting. At the end of the trip, John Stanley admitted he had been wrong about his son. He left, shaking his son's hand, and smiled.

But rumors started to swirl around Gacy.

John's young employees, mostly teenagers, found it strange how their manager only offered the best-looking boys a ride home after work. To onlookers, it seemed typical for Gacy to be driving youngsters around town. They could safely assume he was a kind boss. He made the activity a natural sight, normalized the behavior.

One of those boys was Donald Voorhees.

It was August of 1967 and the sixteen-year-old attended East High School in Waterloo. He was a son of a fellow Jaycee member and probably knew Gacy reasonably well. It was around eleven at night. Gacy's wife and children were away, back at Springfield. John had been out driving when he came across Donald Voorhees. Voorhees was blonde and blue-eyed, well built. He recognized Gacy immediately. According to Gacy, he remembered that Donald Voorhees had been having trouble with his father. He asked the teenager right away how things were going at home. Donald admitted they were only going okay. John immediately made the connection of paternal issues. He offered advice on how to deal with dad problems, but Donald Voorhees wasn't too interested. Gacy switched the conversation.

"So what the hell you doing out here, anyway?" he asked.

"I was at my girlfriend's house. I was walking home. I don't get my license until next year."

The conversation took a turn. It became about girls and dating. John asked a bit about how dating girls was going. He claimed to have been merely trying to relate, and he swears that Donald Voorhees was the one to talk about stag films. Gacy felt an urge to educate the kid in a way his father never had. Donald Voorhees deserved to know, and Gacy invited him back home to watch a few.

They drove back to Gacy's home, where there were no children and no wife to interrupt or question. Gacy led the sixteen-year-old downstairs to his basement, which he spent hours perfecting for hosting stag parties. There he set up the projector and pulled out several of the films. Donald Voorhees quickly became transfixed on the erotic movies playing on the screen. John was less interested in the movie he'd already viewed many times. After a few minutes, Gacy went upstairs to pull a beer out from the kitchen fridge.

He made his way back down the stairs as the movie came to a finish. John asked Donald if he enjoyed the stag films. According to Gacy, Donald answered that it helped open his eyes and teach him more about sex. Perhaps it was the conversation or the film playing, but Gacy felt himself starting to become a bit more aroused. He started talking to Donald about sex, asking if the handsome young man scored many broads. He pushed the questions further, asking Donald more about his sex life, prodding for detail. He noticed how simply talking dirty was making him more aroused as the subject continued. He figured the teenager across from him had to be as well, especially after watching a stag film.

Memories played in his head of that night with Robert Stuart how he had woken up to his friend performing oral sex on him. Nothing was stopping them now. It was a similar situation. John was conveniently home alone.

"You hard?" John asked Donald then. The questions were a bit off-putting and embarrassing. John took the fatherly approach, explaining it was completely natural to be hard after watching a film like that. That was the point. He figured Donald had to be aroused.

"The thing of it is," he explained to the teenager, "read the Kinsey Report, and it shows how most guys your age sometimes go down on a guy. Or have a guy go down on them. It don't mean you're queer; it's part of growing up, becoming a man. You have to have sex with a man before you start having sex with women. Nobody tells you this shit, but it's scientific, and you could read it in reports. So what happens, if you get two guys who are horny and there's no one else around, then you got to take care of each other. You have to help each other out. It's only natural to calm your emotional feelings, or you can actually get sick."

He knew it was complete bullshit, but the way he was selling, hearing the words come out of his mouth, Gacy had almost convinced himself. He was a skilled salesman.

John later recalled that he went first, and when he finished, Voorhees was still a bit reluctant and embarrassed, but John talked him into it.

After what John thought would be nothing more than a one-night stand turned into several times, Donald Voorhees would show up and sleep with John for money. "Each time," John said in an interview, "I thought, well, I'll just give him a little more money, help him get straightened out, and that'll be the last time I see him." But according to Voorhees, Gacy plied him with alcohol to sleep with him, manipulating the young man.

The one-time stand—turned into multiple events—was only the start of Gacy's terror.

It was late August of 1967. Sixteen-year-old Edward Lynch was finishing up a day's work at the Kentucky Fried Chicken. Gacy offered him a ride home, but they had to stop at one of the other restaurants. Lynch climbed into the car, and as they drove, Gacy mentioned stopping home. He told Lynch he had a few stag films they could watch and have a few drinks. Lynch was probably surprised and a little uncomfortable, but it may have been hard to pass up access to alcohol and porn at such a young age.

Down the stairs, Gacy brought Lynch into his rec room where he had taken Voorhees. They started a game of pool. Marlynn Lynch was still at the hospital recovering from the birth of their second child, their baby girl. Gacy began to talk to Lynch about a critical study done about sex. They continued playing pool, and Gacy started to bet money against the young man even when Lynch began to win every game.

Gacy decided then that perhaps they should make the game a bit more interesting. He looked over at the sixteen-year-old and bet a blow job. Lynch was uncomfortable with the offer and told Gacy he was flat out not interested. Gacy began to muddle his words and confuse Lynch. It wasn't exactly a blow job. It was more or less a sexual option aside from whatever amount of money was named. Lynch didn't pay too much attention to the wording. He hadn't lost a game yet. There wasn't a real threat.

And he won that game. When it was over, Gacy asked him what he wanted for winning?

"You can pay me," Lynch answered.

"I'd rather give you a blow job."

Lynch told Gacy to forget the whole thing. He was not interested, and Gacy was his boss, after all. A game of pool was not worth losing his job.

Gacy nonchalantly mentioned the stag films again. He set up the projector and began to play the movies filled with sex scenes. When the movies were finished, Gacy suggested they head upstairs. There he went into the kitchen while Lynch waited around.

When Gacy returned, a knife was clutched in his palm. He lifted it in a threatening manner, demanding Lynch enter the bedroom. With nowhere to turn or go, Lynch was forced down the hallway and into a small bedroom.

Gacy continued pressing forward. Lynch grabbed ahold of the knife-wielding arm of Gacy and tried to push. Grappled, they fell onto the bed. The tip of the blade slid into Lynch's skin. Red blood began to slip out. The two struggled, but Lynch was strong for his age. He managed to roll Gacy over beneath him, and with one strong fist, he landed two hard punches. Gacy dropped the knife, and his breathing grew rapid.

His whole tone turned apologetic. He told Lynch to flip the lights back on then he asked Lynch if he had cut him. With the lights turned on, they examined the wound. It wasn't anything serious, just a puncture through the skin, but Gacy rushed to get a band-aid and applied it over the cut, all while continuing to apologize.

In shock and confusion, Lynch wrote it off as nothing more than horseplay. It was all he could think of to rationalize his boss's erratic behavior. The teenager convinced himself he had overreacted to what was nothing more than Gacy's attempt at a strange joke.

Trying to smooth everything over, Gacy suggested they return downstairs to continue watching another film. But Lynch had had enough. He was ready to get home, away from Gacy and the strange behavior. But Gacy insisted they return to the basement. It was a way of accepting his boss's apology to prove everything was okay. Lynch found himself following Gacy down the steps to the rec room. The film played for ten minutes, and when it was over, Gacy showed Lynch a padlock and chain.

"Stand up a minute. Just let me try something here."

Lynch protested, but Gacy persisted with a non-threatening tone. At sixteen, Lynch was young and gullible. He wanted to keep his job and felt he had to listen to his employer. Lynch placed his hands behind his back, one over the other. Gacy bound them with the chain and locked the padlock in place.

"Is it secure? Can you get loose?" Gacy asked the sixteen-year-old.

Unable to free his hands, Lynch returned to his chair, unsure what exactly the plan was. Gacy suggestively slid onto Lynch's lap, straddling him. Realization set in. Lynch head-butted Gacy with as much force as he could muster. The impact sent Gacy backward, and he stumbled off into another room, returning with a cot on wheels. He opened the mattress up in front of Lynch.

The teenager began to protest, demanding Gacy let him go immediately. But Gacy kept a reassuring, cold voice. He told Lynch everything was going to be okay.

"I want this chain off!" Lynch shouted.

Gacy moved behind him. Perhaps there was a moment of relief for the victim as the chain fell away from his wrist, but it did not last long. Gacy's large hands clamped down, burying Lynch headfirst into the mattress. With Lynch pinned beneath him, he coiled his hands around his throat and began to squeeze. Lynch choked, gasping as the air was locked from his lungs. Burning filled his chest. He could not scream, could not move or fight. He was utterly under Gacy's control. The world around him grew dark as his consciousness faded in and out.

Gacy did not let go, and as his mind began to swim through a thick, dizzy fog, Lynch thought he was in the last moments of his life. John Wayne Gacy was going to kill him then and there. He felt his mind teetering on the brink of eternal darkness. He urinated himself, losing control.

He felt his body being rolled over to the side as the faint light of consciousness began to return to him. At last, the sight of the basement and Gacy came into view. Without a note of remorse, Gacy asked if he was okay. Then he followed with an apology, but Lynch was done. His fists clenched tightly together. He told Gacy it was time to return home.

Days later, Lynch was fired from Kentucky Fried Chicken.

Tears in the Mask

In March of 1968, Donald Voorhees sat across his father at dinner. The subject of John Wayne Gacy came up. Gacy planned to run for president's position within the local Jaycee group and mentioned naming Donald's father as his campaign manager. The talk of Gacy's name sent Donald into a fit of tears. That night he told his father everything about John Wayne Gacy and his secret. Gacy's picture-perfect world as a loving father, dutiful husband, and the most outstanding Jaycee member began to crumble.

Gacy vehemently denied the allegations against him. He demanded a lie detector test on himself to prove his innocence. They took him up on his offer. On May 2, 1968, he was strapped into the lie detector machine and once again asked if he sexually assaulted Voorhees. As expected, John Wayne Gacy failed.

Eight days later, a hard knock fell over the bungalow on Fairlane Street. As everyone else went about their lives, John got out of his chair and opened the front door to come face to face with the police. His heart must have stopped at that moment. Even with all the free food and schmoozing he had put into the police, there was no easy way out. He was arrested then and there for the crime of sodomy.

Gacy had nothing else but to remain steadfast that this was all lies. It was his word against his accusers. The teenagers made up the story, and he was completely innocent. To him, it was nothing more than a conspiracy crafted by Donald's father. He was, after all, next in line to become the President of the Jaycees in Waterloo. It is not unfathomable Voorhees would try something like this. The two never got along, and Voorhees also sought to rise in the club.

As for Lynch, John Wayne Gacy claimed the accusation was a joke. "He says I attacked him with a knife," John later recounted through bouts of laughter. "Then he says he sat down and watched more films with me. Then, get this, then he says he let me chain his hands behind his back. That's real believable after I just supposedly attacked him with the knife. What happened is he got fired and wanted to get back at me."

The gaslighting of his victims seemed to work, and many of his friends believed him. They could see he had political rivals who would want him gone. He and Donald Voorhees's father never got along, and his son was nothing more than a liar. For Gacy, Donald was the reason why he lost his chance at the presidency.

Donald Voorhees's testimony was far different than the way Gacy recalled their relationship. Donald swore in court under oath that Gacy invited him inside, where they performed oral sex upon one another, and Gacy attempted anal on Donald but failed. All of this was forced upon Voorhees. They got together several times; on occasion, they'd meet at a motel, other times at Gacy's home. But Gacy flooded Donald with liquor, molested him, forcing him to recount every detail of their interaction then pay him when finished.

The case dragged on. Gacy had his hand in a lot of the unsavory activity in Waterloo. He was involved in wife swapping, prostitution, and gambling rackets. The prosecutors feared what names might appear on a list if he decided to open his mouth. The case began to fade in the news, but Gacy was unaware. He was vengeful and in fear. He thought there was only one way to secure his freedom. It was extreme, but it was the only solution in his mind.

One of his KFC employees, Russell Schroeder, stood at six feet tall and was well built. Gacy reached out to the eighteen-year-old and offered to help him pay off his car with three hundred dollars if Schroeder beat Donald Voorhees to scare him away from testifying. Russell Schroeder agreed to the offer and talked the details over with Gacy over the next several nights.

Their plan went into action. Schroeder lured Donald Voorhees into Black Hawk Park with the promise of liquor. When they were alone, instead of drinks, Schroeder pummeled Voorhees down to the cold grass and dirt after spraying him with Gacy's can of mace. Donald Voorhees's eyes burned as Schroeder beat him with a thick tree branch. Afraid and confused, Voorhees struggled, crawling to a nearby creek to drench his eyes with cold water.

"Don't testify against John Gacy!" Schroeder shouted as he continued to beat Voorhees, explaining to him why he was there. Voorhees managed to escape in fear, scrambling through the bushes.

When Schroeder returned to Gacy to inform him he had gotten ahold of Voorhees, Gacy seemingly forgot to pay him.

Voorhees wasted no time going to the police with Schroeder's name. And when the police showed up looking for the eighteen-year-old, Schroeder took no convincing to tell the cops everything about Gacy. He had only done the job for the money, which he never received. He had no reason to think he would ever get paid, no reason to hide John's intentions. Now Gacy's fate was sealed.

Gacy's young wife, Marlynn, was left in shock and confusion through it all. She never suspected her husband to have had any sexual relations with teenage boys. Her husband had been nothing more than a good father and husband. When she asked him for the truth, he denied it. It was all still lies.

After Schroeder came forward, Gacy was arrested for suborning perjury and malicious threats to extort. In front of the judge, Gacy continued to proclaim his innocence. He announced he never coerced Schroeder to attack Voorhees to prevent him from testifying.

He was ordered to have a psychiatric evaluation. Until that could be arranged, he was to stay behind bars. Arrested and in prison, he met with a court attorney and several law enforcement officers and told them everything about wife swapping, prostitution, and gambling. All the while, he dropped names, solidifying himself as an important inmate.

With Gacy locked away, investigators began to work on the case, digging into his life. They wanted to convict him on the sodomy charge. It didn't take long to uncover more about the Jaycee chaplain. Several incidents emerged as the investigators progressed.

John Wayne Gacy created a sort of boy's club he hosted out of his basement for his employees and their friends. He charged the young men a monthly fee. With payment, the teenagers were treated to free-flowing drinks and rounds of pools. He encouraged them to drink as much as they wanted. After a game of pool, Gacy would every now and then bet a blow job. And when the boys refused to follow through, Gacy merely laughed. It was nothing more than their boss's weird sense of humor. If that didn't work, he used the ploy he was doing work for science. While most of his victims during this time remain unknown, investigators found several leads.

Richard Westphal, a seventeen-year-old working at one of Gacy's KFC restaurants for two years, was a part of the club. At times, he would help Gacy with remodeling his house. The two would work on various projects, and sometimes Gacy would joke about Westphal having sex with Marlynn.

"If I ever catch you in bed with my wife, you'll owe me a blow job," he'd sometimes turn the joke into a threat.

In January of 1967, Westphal worked on the bar in Gacy's basement rec room. It was a cold, dark winter night in Waterloo, and it had gotten rather late. Gacy invited Westphal to stay the night instead of driving out. Tired, Westphal accepted the invitation, climbing into bed for what he thought would be a typical night, until the door opened. Marlynn entered the dark bedroom. She crawled into the bed beside him, and they had sex. For Westphal, it was a strange experience as well as his first time. When they finished, John barged into the room, turning on the light as if he was waiting for the perfect moment to pounce.

"See, I caught you. Now, you owe me a blow job," Gacy affirmed. Not for a moment was he upset with the seventeen-year-old for sleeping with Marlynn. In fact, he was victorious. Confused and ridden with guilt for sleeping with his employer's wife, Gacy would finally receive what he wanted. Days later, Westphal was pressured into giving his "payment."

Other boys talked about Gacy's strange claims. Apparently, he declared that the governor of Illinois hired Gacy to conduct secret sexual experiments in the field of homosexuality. He even forged a false certificate for proof of his work and paid the boys to engage in the experiments. He encouraged them to get drunk. When he was done with the experiment, Gacy was sure to pay the boy five dollars for their work from, what he called, the governor's secret fund.

Awaiting his trial, John was moved from jail to the Psychopathic Hospital, where he stayed for seventeen days and underwent various tests. There, he told them about his heart condition and about his episodes of blacking out. The doctors ran a series of tests to back up his claims. The specialists couldn't find proof of any of these conditions. There was no brain trauma nor heart condition. Aside from being overweight, John Wayne Gacy was in excellent health.

And when the psychiatrists and psychologists interviewed Gacy, they listened to him recount his side of the story. His recollection vastly differed from the witnesses. To many of the hospital workers, Gacy came across as somewhat of a con man. He was aggressive to those he thought of as weak and submissive and kind to the ones in a position of authority.

When his evaluation was complete, the doctors believed John was a bright individual and had high social intelligence, which he used to manipulate those around him. He constantly saw himself as a victim, was always able to provide an alibi for what happened to him and why. He was diagnosed with "sociopathic personality disturbance, antisocial reaction." The crimes committed by his hands were done by choice and made out of freewill. Choices that were most likely to be repeated and treatment was extremely unlikely to help. They believed there was no treatment for him, and these tendencies would recur.

John appeared before the court. When the judge read the guilty verdict, Gacy's knees grew weak. He almost passed out in front of the whole courtroom. But he maintained his stoic demeanor until leaving. In long, black robes and serious eyes, the judge told Gacy, "The particular pattern you seem to have chosen is to seek out teenage boys and get them involved in sexual misbehavior." He was given the full sentence of ten years at Iowa State Reformatory for Men.

John Stanley appeared in court alongside his wife. They stood and watched that day as their only son was sentenced. He openly wept in the courtroom. It was the only time his family had seen him cry. He sobbed, but John never saw.

On the same day, Marlynn filed for divorce. Her father had been right all along. John would never see his two children again. And until the day he died, he saw himself as nothing more than a victim in Waterloo.

Return to Chicago

John Wayne Gacy became inmate 26525 but losing his name, freedom, wife, and children weren't going to keep a man from doing his work. He flourished living in the systematic routine of prison. John delved into the social scene of prison life. He sought out to befriend first-timers who were locked up for nonviolent offenses and did everything in his power to stay away from the gay men. He made it known how much he hated "fruit pickers."

He found his spot working the kitchen and worked his way up to the number one cook with several years of restaurant experience. One of the inmates Gacy befriended described him as someone who "enjoyed considerable power because of his control over one of the necessities of an institution, which is food." The kitchen allowed him to give certain inmates and staff special meals. Gacy was determined to set himself up.

And it wasn't long until Gacy walked around Men's Reformatory at Anamosa, cigar hanging out of his mouth, white shirt on instead of the uniform, showing off the level of privilege he had earned. Wherever he was, in his hand he carried a black briefcase, a sign of his work. He was a businessman through and through. And even in the prison walls, Gacy continued his dutiful work of gathering new Jaycee members. He went on to win the Spoke Award, the Spark Plug Award, and Jaycee Sound Citizen Award while behind bars. To the inmates, he walked around as the hardest worker they knew, a real hustler. That was how Gacy positioned himself.

His efforts were not to benefit only himself. Gacy worked tirelessly for his father to clear their family's name. Maybe the moment his father cried, the one and only time, struck a chord with Gacy.

Unfortunately, John Stanley died on Christmas Day in 1969 from cirrhosis of the liver. Years of overindulging in alcohol led to his death. When he was sick, Gacy wasn't able to leave prison to visit him. A pain and burden that weighed down on inmate 26525. A pain that haunted Gacy for the rest of his life. He never spoke a bad word about his father. He described him later: "My dad was domineering. He had a different set of values but also a very stern individual. My dad drank a lot, and when he drank a lot, he was abusive to my mother and to me. But I never swung at my dad because I loved him for what he stood for."

John applied for early parole, and after only serving eighteen months of a ten-year sentence, it was granted. In the eyes of his jailers, he was an outstanding inmate and had thoroughly proven himself.

He was once again a free man.

The day he was released, he had dinner with Charles Hill and his wife. They spoke about prison and how rough it had been on Gacy. He choked up when he spoke about his father's passing. The conversation bled deep into the night. Gacy vowed to Hill that he would never set foot in prison again.

Away from the past, back to Chicago, Gacy returned to live with his mother in a condo his father purchased and paid off. He grabbed a job at Bruno's Restaurant and Lounge on Wells Street. It was a fresh start, and Gacy was back to dating and having consensual sex.

Every now and then, a man named James Hanley would come into Bruno's with the other police officers who frequented the spot. Gacy went out of his way to befriend the officers and speak with them. He still held cops in high regard. But Hanley stood out to him more than the others. Gacy assumed he was undercover or a detective working tough cases. They didn't speak much, just a few words. Strong and muscular, James Hanley sort of exuded everything Gacy was not. And it was James Hanley who Gacy would embody later in life to commit foul acts of murder.

In the early winter of 1971, Gacy made his way to the Greyhound Bus Terminal at Clark and Randolph Streets in Chicago's Loop. It was a busy hub—one of the busiest in the world. Thousands of people came and went, passing through on their travels. Gacy knew this is where he could stop to pick up sex workers and young men.

He couldn't help himself; the old ways returned. Gacy approached the bus station. A young man caught his eye. He stopped the car. He probably used his best salesman voice, luring the young victim in hopes to relieve some sexual tension. John Wayne Gacy offered to take him back to his place. The boy accepted, not knowing what the man truly had in mind. When they were alone in the house, Gacy forced himself upon him. And on February 12, 1971, a mere eight months after receiving parole, Gacy was arrested and charged with "assault on a sexual deviate."

Gacy picked the kid up who was a hitchhiker, and when the teenager offered sexual favors, Gacy became so enraged he kicked the kid out of his car. How dare he think that Gacy would be into such acts. But it was all dropped when the teenager failed to show up for court. Somehow his information from Waterloo never made it into the hands of the Chicago police. Luck kept him from returning to the place he vowed never to step foot in again.

His freedom was almost taken from him with that one self-indulgence. Not to waste any more of his time, Gacy knew he needed to shift careers. Working as a cook was nothing more than a dead-end job. He decided to make a switch and started PDM Contractors: Painting, Decorating, and Maintenance. Parole required Gacy to be in by 10 pm, but his parole officer was a bit lenient with the curfew because of his hard work ethic.

In July of 1971, Gacy drove down Clark and Broadway to the bus terminal. He spotted a young man and introduced himself. Mickel Reid had just moved from Ohio out to Chicago. He was new in town and unemployed, currently looking for a job. They quickly struck up a conversation, and Gacy started telling him all about his business and the type of work involved. He stressed the massive amounts of money a man could make in that line of work. A natural salesman, always selling a pitch.

The conversation continued, and Gacy invited the new arrival over to his house. The naive Midwesterner accepted, and they ended up returning to Gacy's home. The talk turned into more than words, and eventually, the two of them had sex. Gacy paid Reid for it after.

They continued to meet, discussing a partnership in PDM. The business was starting to take off now, and Gacy needed the help and more space.

He found himself a lovely two-bedroom ranch at 8213 West Summerdale Avenue, which his mother agreed to help with the financing. It was a quiet, family-friendly neighborhood with well-kept lawns and quiet streets. Like the previous four owners, Gacy made a few alterations. It was a substantial construction tract home from the 1950s, well built. The garage was perfect for keeping his tools, and the crawl space underneath could be extra storage if it would stop flooding. He made a rec room for himself that was once a playroom by adding a sliding glass door to the back. He also had another pool table and a bar, which was always stocked full of a variety of options. A red stop sign hung above on the wall.

As their work relationship progressed, Mickel Reid moved in. The two continued to work together. Mostly painting and house maintenance, nothing extreme. Sometimes they would sleep with one another, and other times they would have small arguments over money. Money was a bit tight in the beginning. Gacy made ends meet by stealing things for the company.

An argument between Reid and Gacy began one day, one about money, which was not out of the ordinary. It took an unusual turn when they decided to rob a house. Gacy drove Reid out to a desolate area. Reid got out of the car, but when he looked, he saw in Gacy's hand a tire iron. He asked Gacy, who had stopped dead in his tracks, why he brought the tire iron.

"In case there's trouble," Gacy responded. Reid looked around. They were completely alone. Confusion fell over him. There was no reason to believe they would run into trouble. He no longer wanted to break in, and so they returned home and began to unload equipment.

In the shadowy thickness of the night, it was dark in the garage. The lights had gone out overhead, and Gacy asked Reid to get some fuses beneath the workbench. Reid bent down on his hands and knees. Suddenly, the hard metal of a hammer came down onto his head. "I stayed down a couple of seconds, and I stood up, and I saw that John was looking like he was going to hit me again. I put my hand up to stop his hand from coming back down, and at the same time, I asked him what he was doing or why he wanted to hit me," Reid later recalled.

A strange look hovered there in Gacy's eyes. A moment passed as they stood staring at one another. All the while, Reid was dumbstruck as to why his partner would suddenly attack him. Gacy's expression lightened as he lowered the hammer and began to apologize profusely. Gacy brought Reid inside and began to patch his head, continuing the stream of apologies for the next hour.

Reid never understood why Gacy came at him. He wondered if it was because of money. They would roughhouse at times, but that was just fooling around.

The next day Mickel Reid moved out of Gacy's home. Gacy found himself once again without a partner and alone, but that didn't last very long.

At the end of that same year, Carole Hoff went through a divorce. She was left with her two daughters, a three-year-old and one-year-old. It was difficult trying to support herself and two little girls as a single working mother. Growing up, she spent a lot of her time at the Gacy's house as a teenager, like a part of the family. Karen Gacy was her good school friend, and as an adult, she started spending more and more time at the house. She felt comfortable around John. In her eyes, Gacy was "a very warm, understanding person, very easy to talk to, knew a lot of things. It was very easy to just listen to him. I always felt he knew what he was talking about. And I met a lot of interesting people through John." He had connections and scored tickets to the Black Hawk hockey games.

Gacy told her all about the cop friends he had made. And around children, Carole couldn't help but notice how soft and gentle he was with her two little ones. The girls called him "Daddy" even before the two were married.

She wasn't sure if it was ever true love, but Carole was comfortable with John. He had just gotten out of prison, and she, a divorce. When the dates became increasingly serious, he told her about spending time in Iowa prison for showing teenagers porn. As they progressed, he told her he was bisexual. She thought it was a joke, and so their relationship continued. She figured there was nothing to worry about. John had made it known how much he loathed gay men. She explained later, "He told me he was a bisexual. At first I didn't understand what a bisexual was. So he explained it to me and I just kind of looked at him. I said, 'How do you know you're a bisexual? How can you just say, 'This is what I am'?"

His charm and kindness were enough to win her over. They found mutual comfort within one another.

John Wayne Gacy's life continued moving forward. The arrest from earlier that year never made it to the Iowa Board of Parole. Gacy was released from parole that October, and forty-five days before Gacy's first kill, he was granted full rights as a citizen.

To the outside world looking in, John Wayne Gacy had fully turned his life around. He was constantly moving, hauling in loads of concrete or drywall for the next project on his house. They watched with interest wondering what next addition he would make. Aside from a wave now and then, Edward J. and Lillie Grexa hadn't spoken to their new neighbor until Christmas Eve, when they heard a loud knock at their front door.

There stood John Wayne Gacy, beaming with a massive smile, and in his arms, he clutched a box full of fruit. He introduced himself then, letting them know he figured they would need the fruit for the six children they had. With all the neighborly warmth Gacy mustered, he invited them over for Christmas dinner. The Grexas were happy to accept the invitation.

Christmas evening was spent with laughter and great food. Lillie Grexa brought over a tray of cookies to share with everyone. They met his family as well as his girlfriend, Carole. They were pleased to find their new neighbors were kind, family-centered people.

For the Grexas, as they headed back home that Christmas night, walking over the few feet of lawn that separated their homes, they began a friendship that would last seven years. Many neighbors wished to have a relationship as welcoming and friendly, and the two houses continued to be a part of each other's lives for nearly a decade.

Carole later mentioned that every year around the Christmas Holidays, Gacy would make the trip to Maryhill Cemetery. There he would visit his father's grave. He would speak to his father and return home in tears, visibly upset.

The first year, 1971, was the worst and most dramatic of the cemetery visits. John Wayne Gacy came home after the cemetery visit with tears streaming down his face. He could not stop the sobs as the guilt of disappointing his father weighed down and being unable to visit him one last time. His behavior reinforced the idea to their neighbors that Gacy valued family and home life above all else.

The two families established a friendship over that Christmas dinner. Little did they know, in a little over one week, John Wayne Gacy would begin a murderous rampage over the streets of Chicago that would not stop until he claimed the lives of over thirty victims.

The Stabbing

New Year's Day 1971, Gacy drove Carole to Kennicott, where her two little girls stayed with their grandmother. When they said their goodbyes, he told them they wouldn't be able to see each other for the next few days because Aunt Pearl had passed that night.

That same evening he went to his Aunt Ethel's house, where his mother had been staying. There was little talk of Aunt Pearl's passing, and the evening was spent drinking and playing cards. Aunt Ethel was the type to make strong drinks, and she didn't hold back when she poured a scotch for Gacy. He hadn't intended on getting drunk, but his family was full of talkers. If he didn't pay attention, his aunt would keep filling the glass. It wasn't Gacy's fault he got so inebriated.

A little after midnight, the party began to teeter off. Gacy insisted he drive his mother home, but she fought him on that. She refused to get in the car with someone who had been drinking. Gacy tried to put up an argument, but he gave in then and left. It was a cold winter's night in Chicago, and the air was bitter. He climbed into his car, but he knew then he wasn't tired. He figured he'd drive down to the civic center and look at the ice sculptures.

But he knew well enough, the bus terminal was close to the civic center. He drove by the ice sculptures that glistened in the lights. When he was finished, he returned to his car. Passerbys walked around, and from where Gacy was at, he could spot the bus terminal. He drove over to it.

There were no witnesses to verify the story. But John Wayne Gacy told it over many times in interviews.

On the brisk winter night, his car pulled up to the station. He rolled down the window. His breath gathered in wisps of fog as he exhaled. In his line of sight, a teenager waited on the bench. He asked the boy sitting at the station what he was doing. The somewhat scrawny teenager with light blonde hair looked up. He had on a plaid shirt and a pair of Levi's.

The kid told John that he was doing nothing and had twelve hours to kill.

"You wanna drive around?" John asked him. "You wanna see the sights?" Gacy put on the air that he was a tour guide, taking the kid under his wing, showing him the sights of Chicago. They drove north first. He showed him Old Town/New Town. "This here is the gay part of town," Gacy told the boy. The subject of sex came up then, and Gacy asked if the teenager had ever been with a man. They talked it over. As John listened, he deduced the kid was inexperienced with being with a man but was a bit curious about it all.

The boy grew hungry, and they ended up back at Gacy's Summerdale ranch. The house was empty. Gacy went into the kitchen, pulling out a big slab of meat, he used a butcher knife to slice it for sandwiches. Leaving the knife out on the counter, Gacy brought the sandwiches out to the living room, where the kid sat waiting near the bar. Next, Gacy made a few drinks for them. All Gacy had was a beer, but the transient teen wanted 190 proof alcohol. Gacy figured he was trying to show off or prove he was a man.

The topic of sex came up once again, and they performed oral sex on one another. When they were finished, Gacy was tired. He told the kid he could sleep over for the night, and then they could head back to the bus station in the morning. Gacy said goodnight, then laid down in bed.

It was around four in the morning when, from his sleep, something jolted Gacy awake. He wasn't quite sure what it was. Perhaps a sound or maybe something more ominous—a feeling. But when he came to, he saw the kid standing in the doorway. The lights of the house backlit his figure, but Gacy made out the butcher knife clutched in the palm of his hand. The boy slowly moved forward. Gacy felt as if he was living an actual dream. He was confused, unsure what to do, and he claimed he pushed the teenager down, knocking him back in self-defense. Grappled, they fell on top of one another.

The blade cut Gacy. He couldn't remember if words were spoken, but if they had been, he figured he was demanding to know why he was being attacked. The wound on Gacy's arm was now bright red with blood. They struggled between one another for the knife. Gacy hadn't really stabbed him. "He just fell on the floor, and I think he fell on the knife. He stuck himself with the knife because I had hold of his hand and I had turned the knife inward, toward him, toward his stomach or his chest, and he fell on it, and I fell on top of him." Other times, Gacy recalled that he might have stabbed four or five times and that the kid was shirtless.

When the conflict ended, knife in his hand, Gacy went to the bathroom. He washed the blood from the metal blade then proceeded to clean himself. From the bedroom, he heard gurgles that wouldn't stop. He moved through the house, returning the knife to its proper place. He moved to the bathroom, then back to the kitchen, waiting for the gurgling noise to stop. The young man struggled to fight for his last breaths. Finally, the sounds stopped, and silence fell over. Gacy returned to the bedroom where the young man now laid silent and dead. Blood collected onto the floor in a red, shining pool.

Gacy should have called the police, but he couldn't. As soon as he phoned them up, they would find out he had a record in Iowa. In his mind, he'd been framed once before; it could easily happen again. He had to take care of the situation on his own. There was no other option.

First, he cleaned up the blood. Then he dragged the body to the bedroom closet, opened the trap door leading to the crawl space, and shoved the body down. He set the board back in its place.

When investigators removed the body from the crawl space years later, it was the ninth one pulled. The body was nothing more than a skeleton. But pathologists found visible traces of multiple stab wounds in the chest. It was the only victim out of the thirty-three stabbed to death by Gacy, and the first of his murders.

He knew his mother would be coming home that day. He inspected the house for traces of any more blood. He picked his mother up from his Aunt Ethel's, and together they attended the wake for his Aunt Pearl.

Joanne noticed the cut on his arm. Concerned, she asked what happened to her brother. He lied. "I did it cutting carpet in the kitchen this morning," he said. "I slipped with the knife." She worried about the wound. It was a serious cut. Deep. Joanne had studied to be a nurse and urged her brother to get medical care for it. Surrounded by family and friends that were worried and concerned for Gacy, he knew then what he may have always suspected. John Wayne Gacy could kill someone, and no one would see him differently. It was his secret.

After Gacy got stitches, he and his mother returned home. He didn't have much time until the young man from the bus terminal's body began to decompose and fill the house with an awful stench. Conveniently for Gacy, he worked in construction. He used his work-related skills to cover up his first murder.

He went down into the crawl space where there were only two feet of headroom. In the cramped, dark space, bent over, John Wayne Gacy dug a shallow grave for the teenage boy, who never made it home after the holidays. The first of many.

A few months later, Gacy and Carole announced their engagement. Marion Gacy moved out of the house then. She wanted the couple to enjoy their life together without anyone else's input. They set the date for July 1, 1972. Gacy's violent behavior went unnoticed. That is, until nine days before the wedding, he was arrested. The charge was aggravated battery and reckless conduct.

John Wayne Gacy had been cruising in Chicago's north side, club district. He found a young man and flashed a badge, claiming that he was a police officer. He ordered the teen into his car and forced him to perform oral. With the young man trapped in the car, Gacy drove north for another twenty miles. He was resting, eager to receive another blow job. But the second time he stopped the car, the young man threw the door open and bolted. Gacy chased him down in the car, trying to run the young man down.

But the charges were mysteriously dropped. That night became nothing more than a blip in John's timeline. Their marriage ceremony could continue as planned.

Gacy and Carole were married at St. Paul's Lutheran Church. Being Catholic, Gacy would have preferred a ceremony within his own religion, but he had been divorced. The Catholic church did not approve of divorce and looked down upon it greatly. John could avoid the religious scrutiny by marrying at the church right down the street from his home.

They had the reception in the backyard of Gacy's home. Kielbasa and sauerkraut, potato salad, and coleslaw were served. The Grexas helped prepare the food. They were excited for the neighbor who had quickly become a close friend. Around one hundred and fifty guests came to celebrate the nuptials—none of them aware of the boy's body rotting beneath the home.

And John and Carole made love and slept in the bedroom where that boy laid on the floor months earlier, taking his last breaths as he bled out.

In the early part of their marriage, the only thing that started to bother Carole was the house's smell. Otherwise, John was a king and a warm lover. Her husband was manly but not overly so, and he was terrific with the two girls. "He was a very good father to my girls," Carole later said. "Never beat them, whipped them. He very seldom hollered. I was the one that was hollering, not him." They returned from their two-day honeymoon to Wisconsin, and Gacy went back to work. Carole stayed at home with her daughters. The foul odor grew worse and worse as the summer days grew hotter. There were mice upstairs, so she set traps, but that didn't explain how the smell was coming from beneath the house. And when the crawl space flooded, it reeked. Even the Grexas noticed the musty odor that lingered in the walls.

In the utility room, she later described, "There were a lot of little black—I don't know if they were little gnats, but they almost looked like flies at times." She figured there were flies laying eggs on all the dead mice in the crawl space. Blowflies detect the scent of decomposing cadaver and will deposit their eggs on the open wounds. One fly can lay up to 250 eggs within one day. She wanted to contact an exterminator, but Gacy told her not to worry.

"I'll go down there and set a few traps," he told her. Gacy was always ready to handle the chores of his home. Still insisting he would fix it. He had to worry about someone happening upon the corpse of the boy he murdered not long ago.

"John, if the mice are dead, how are they going to get in the traps?" Carole responded.

After a trip out of town, he informed her he had laid a concrete slab down. It helped, just like when he covered the front of the house in brick, blocking two of the crawl space vents, preventing the odor from seeping through the home. That helped as well. But as long as Carole lived there, she smelled the faint, sewer-like scent ever present, lingering. It was the scent of death.

The smell did not keep their first year from being a great time in the marriage. The second, however, was the opposite. Gacy quit Brunos to invest his time and energy into PDM. It became an obsession. He left for work early, running home in the afternoon, only to work later hours. Sometimes he would head off in the middle of the night for business-related projects.

To Carole, it appeared her husband only needed about an hour of sleep to none. He would come home and hop in the shower. She assumed he crawled into the bed beside her, but then he would get dressed and tell her he had "a few bids, check a building, or talk to someone. It always had to do with work, and he'd leave maybe somewhere around anywhere from twelve-thirty, or maybe it was one or after one. And he'd be gone all night," Carole described.

Sex between them stopped altogether. Gacy was too tired to engage and became less and less interested.

But more was shifting. Carole's view of her gentle and warm husband was changing.

Once, while cleaning beneath the sink, she found magazines of naked men, bloody and gruesome with disturbing images. She found a pair of silk panties with male semen dried on them in the bedsheets. Another was in the dresser and under the bed.

Upset, she confronted Gacy with them. He grew defensive, claiming they weren't his. He would not stand to be accused in his own home. The argument grew. Carole looked at her husband. "Jag off!" she called him. Rage flew through Gacy. He shot out his hand, clamping down hard on her wrist, and threw Carole across the room. It was the only time he was ever violent with her. The term "jag off," Carole knew, would send her husband into a blind and violent rage.

Their marriage did not improve, and with what little time he had to spend, he did not dedicate it to his new family. No, he spent his free time working on the house. He puttered around in the garage. It was his space. Carole and the girls were not allowed to be in there.

As the business continued to grow, Gacy slept many nights on the couch. His work kept him out of the house until four or six in the morning. It left Carole feeling uneasy. He left her home alone often.

She couldn't sleep one night. She heard the sound of Gacy's car pulling up into the driveway. She got up then and headed into the living room. There she sank into the couch and turned the television on to wait. The only light illuminating her was the dim glow of the television. She heard Gacy in the garage, rummaging about. And when the door swung open, Carole's unexpected presence startled Gacy. He asked her what she was doing. She simply told him she couldn't sleep. Confused and taken aback, Gacy acted as though he was merely grabbing something from inside and then headed back out to the car. Carole watched, peering out the window. "He went right back out to the garage, and as he went out there, I looked through the curtains, and

I saw a young boy, blond hair, get in the car, and he hurried up and drove off."

She waited until he was gone and decided it was finally time she would inspect the garage. Even though she shared this home with her husband, he had been clear; she was never to enter. She opened the door. A red light shined a dim eerie glow on the space. There was also a mirror and a blanket.

Carole never confronted her husband about the garage. She didn't want it to lead to another violent argument. She feared accusations would lead to another violent outburst.

But it was only a matter of time until she found out her husband was sleeping with teenage boys.

Run Away

In the summer of 1973, John came home beaten and bruised. The injuries were horrible enough that his wife immediately worried and asked questions. One of his disgruntled employees jumped him. John Wayne Gacy fabricated some story hoping his wife would buy the lie.

He told her it was merely a dispute over money. According to Gacy, the employee was upset about a withheld check. "The kid was painting some steps," John later explained in an interview, "and he did a piss-poor job on them: paint running, thick and thin spots. So, I told him to paint the steps over before he went home. Well, he went home and never did the steps. Now, I had to do that job, because I wasn't going to get paid if the customer wasn't happy. Then he wants his check. For the work I did. So that's what the fight was about."

Outside the house, the young employee waited for Gacy, who was on his way out of work, coming directly home as any dutiful husband would. John was innocent, doing nothing out of the ordinary. Well, the boy attacked without warning, catching her poor husband off-guard. The teenager was wild, swinging punches. All Gacy could do was crawl up onto the pavement and wait until the assault ended. He didn't fight back. How could he? His mother-in-law had been staying at the house and came rushing out to intervene.

But Carole heard a different tale about her husband.

John wanted to inspect a land plot in Florida he recently purchased and invited the young man along to join him on the drive. The first night they spent in Florida, Gacy raped the employee. Terrified and upset, the employee spent the rest of the trip sleeping on the beach. The dispute was not over a miscommunication or lack of work. John was not an innocent victim attacked by an angry teenager. No, the employer raped the boy. He was defending himself. Frightened and desperate, that was why the employee attacked John.

These accusations came as no surprise to Carole. She was watching her new marriage disintegrate before her, and she was powerless. Nothing made it more clear to her than the night of Mother's Day three years into their marriage.

The couple celebrated the day together and ended the evening in bed. Things began to become intimate, but it stopped. Gacy looked at Carole dead in the eyes and told her that this would be the last time they would ever have sex. Carole wanted to write that off as nothing more than a bizarre joke. But Gacy's serious tone didn't shift, and she realized then how serious her husband was.

"How," Carole insisted, "how can you say—?"

"Because I did."

"But . . . you've got to be kidding."

"No, this is the last time."

He claimed to have tried with her over the last year. But demands from work and life were too much. He described crawling into bed after working sixteen-hour shifts to try and have sex with his wife. But he knew sex with a woman took tenderness and love like how his mother taught him. There was kissing and passion, not like animal sex with men, and he was far too exhausted for such romantic activity.

The way John saw it, having his mother-in-law move in with his small family was the reason why his marriage crumbled. He accused Carole's mother of "planting seeds" of separation in his wife, causing strife and giving Carole a reason to doubt her ever hardworking husband for working late into the night and never being home.

"Carole, I swear, as God is my witness, that I am not having relations with any females, okay?"

"Then," John later claimed Carole said, "you're having them with boys."

John continued to say there was no one else in his life, but Carole saw who John hired. She saw how he would bring teenage boys into their garage late at night. Gacy claimed the stress of his family's doubt and pestering weighed down on him to the point of giving him a stroke. And he pointed it all back to his mother-in-law for inciting suspicion. He moved his mother-in-law out of his house in 1974. But to John, her goal of ruining their marriage had been accomplished. It was clear. Carole did not trust her husband. "Once," John described, "I think Carole saw me smoke some marijuana with one of the employees out by the garage. I never saw what they got out of it, but it was after work. And that was the way they liked to relax, and we were talking. So, Carole says, 'If you're not having sex, you're dealing drugs in the garage.' Because she thought I was going out at night to deal drugs then."

Gacy reasoned that if his wife was going to accuse him of sleeping with boys, then he might as well do the damn thing. What did it matter? If she thought he was doing it anyway, what difference did it make if he actually did it then? With that strange rationalization of his behavior, John slept with several young men working for him.

One was a fourteen-year-old, working part-time for PDM at the rate of three dollars an hour. John gave him the Kinsey report spiel as he had to Voorhees, knowing the younger boys were easiest to manipulate. When doubt arose, he simply had them suck his thumb first, proving oral on a man was no different. The older ones required far more elaborate traps.

The way he saw it, having sex with men was like masturbation. He never cheated on his wife. It was animal sex, something primal. There was no love like there was with Carole. Ten dollars spent on a boy walking the streets wasn't love. It was quick and mindless.

It didn't take long before he sought out more teenagers to satisfy his carnal desires. In early 1975, John Wayne Gacy created Jack Hanley's character to peruse the streets after dark. His inspiration came from the tough cop who occasionally visited Bruno's when Gacy was a chef there. Jack Hanley was everything

Gacy wasn't. Tough, strong, and most importantly, Jack Hanley hated gay men. Under this false identity of an undercover cop, Gacy stalked young men and forced them into his car. He spoke in a deeper, gruff voice and handled the young men with no-nonsense, often flashing a fake badge to get their attention and obedience.

In May, he met Tony Antonucci. Gacy was doing a contracting job at the Antonuccis' residence. Tony was fifteen years old and looking for a job. With an athletic build and standing around six feet, he'd be a perfect fit for the hard labor John required of his employees. Gacy offered him one at PDM for three dollars an hour. Together they worked through the early summer. They laid tile and did electrical and plumbing. It was when they worked alone in the evening that Gacy would start to make advances. One night while working inside an office, he offered Tony a blow job; the fifteen-year-old refused. Then, when sitting on a couch, Gacy offered Tony whiskey, encouraging the young man to drink. He brought up the topic of homosexuality and even offered upwards of fifty to a hundred dollars. All Tony could do was continue turning down Gacy's sexual advances.

Gacy simply made the whole situation come off as a sort of exam. He wanted to know as a business owner if he could trust his employees to have morals. But then, his large hands grabbed at Tony's crotch and buttocks. That did it. Tony had enough. He grabbed a nearby chair, raising it overhead, ready to swing down. Gacy burst out into a laugh. It was nothing but a joke. He pointed out that Antonucci should have said stop if he didn't want to horse around. Later, while out grabbing burgers, Gacy reaffirmed he was simply testing his employee, as any good boss does. He couldn't have people who would "break under pressure."

One month later, in July, Tony hurt his foot while working with Gacy. A nail had gone right through the bottom of his shoe into his foot. With his mother and father on vacation, Tony remained at home by himself, healing. One of those nights, he casually sat on the couch. Tony was probably watching TV or listening to music when a hard knock sounded on the door. Of course, Gacy had stopped by.

Antonucci figured his boss was being thoughtful and caring by checking in on him. The whole situation was unusual for a wholesome check-in. It was late, nearing midnight, and in his hand was a bottle of wine. He explained it off by telling Tony that he had just been to a party in the neighborhood and figured he'd stop by.

Teenagers are not known for turning down free alcohol; so, Tony welcomed him in. The two began to drink. Shortly into their beverages, Gacy brought up how he watched stag films at the party. He even had the movies and projector all conveniently in his car. Gacy began persistently asking the teenager about watching them. Finally, Antonucci gave in and said, "Okay."

Gacy hauled in the projector and set it up. The films were men and women engaging in sex. The man and teenager watched, sipping on their wine. The porn ended. Gacy reached out for Tony, grabbing him. They started to wrestle. Horse playing around. Nothing serious. Mostly headlocks or armlocks. Tony was on the Gordon Technical High School's wrestling team, and he made sure not to embarrass Gacy as they roughhoused. But the mood shifted when the cold metal of handcuffs brushed Tony's left arm. Immediately he swung in defense, but Gacy was ready. Within minutes Tony was handcuffed, arms behind his back. In one solid hit, Gacy knocked Tony down.

Gacy began unbuttoning the boy's shirt on the ground, face-up and helpless, then he unbuckled his pants, pulling them down to his knees. No words were spoken. All Tony could do was watch in confusion and horror as his boss left him, half-undressed on the living room floor while Gacy made a trip into the kitchen. Luckily, the right cuff wasn't on so tight. Once the teenager knew Gacy was out of sight, Tony worked to slip his right arm free. Careful not to make a sound or tip-off that he escaped, he remained down on the ground, both arms still pressed behind himself.

Gacy returned to the room. Not wasting another second, Tony lurched up off the floor and bolted. Only weighing around one hundred and seventy-five pounds, Tony was not heavier than Gacy, who was well over two hundred, but he knew how to tackle. He was now fighting for his life. His shoulders slammed into Gacy's knees, throwing him down. He managed to snag the handcuff key off Gacy and thus turned the tables. He slapped the handcuffs onto his boss. This time it was Gacy lying face down with both hands cuffed behind his back. Tony held him down, then got up, leaving his employer face down on the floor.

"Not only are you the only one that got out of the cuffs, you got them on me," Gacy said. A strange feeling crawled up Tony's skin. At that time, he didn't understand what they meant or the horrifying truth behind them. Bound by his young employee, Gacy remained calm and rational. Little was said. It was agreed Gacy would leave immediately. Tony let Gacy go, and he just walked out the door.

Tony worked for PDM for an additional eight months.

But only one week after Tony handcuffed Gacy, another young employee did not escape.

At sixteen years old, John Butkovich thought he had snatched up a great job opportunity. He hadn't finished high school but working at PDM provided good pay. For a young single person, it was enough to live off. Gacy described him as a "fast learner." Even Carole noticed how sweet he was. He visited Summerdale on occasion, playing with her two young girls. Carole referred to Gacy and Butkovich as "Big John" and "Little John."

Over time, she noticed how John would get in fights with his employees. Often, it turned into horsing around or wrestling matches. Carole thought Gacy was too tough on the kids, but he saw it as keeping them in line. Often the fight was about money or payment. Carole later described how "Big John always felt that the boys would end up putting too many hours on the card anyway; so, it was a little argument over the hours that Little John did spend on the job that Big John didn't think he did."

July 31, 1975, Carole was gone on a trip visiting family. According to Gacy, Butkovich arrived at his home late at night with some friends, demanding money for a carpet job they had worked on together. The conversation grew heated. Gacy was able to smooth over the confrontation, and they reached an agreement. They smoked some weed and drank. Gacy over-indulged and got drunk. Stoned and intoxicated from the multiple glasses of scotch, John passed out in the leather armchair; Butkovich and his friends had left.

These occurrences seemed to repeat themselves. John Wayne Gacy drifted out into a dark, mindless sleep and came to in his car, driving down Chicago's streets. Except for, he was no longer John Wayne Gacy. Now he was Jack Hanley, a tough, no-bullshit cop.

He took the same route where he knew the gay men hung out. The area was populated mostly by poor kids and hustlers. That was what Jack Hanley wanted. The ones who were desperate, willing to work for the money.

That night, he hadn't been searching for Butkovich in particular. He claimed it was merely circumstantial he found him while driving. He waved at the teenager. Jack Hanley's persona left, and John was himself again. He could tell Butkovich wanted to talk. He hopped into Gacy's car, and the two started driving. Both drunk. Butkovich wanted to keep drinking. So, Gacy brought him home to Summerdale. There they could keep the night going.

They walked into the empty home. Gacy lit up a joint. He liked to keep them pre-rolled and stored in the fridge for the boys. Ready to go at a moment's notice. The two had another drink. Gacy claimed this is the drink that put Butkovich over the edge. According to John's story, anger suddenly came over the boy.

"You shithead, gimme my check! I could pound the crap out of you right now!" Butkovich shouted, enraged. Gacy remained calm as he spoke back. "You know, I got a heart condition. No way you couldn't kick my ass. Just the excitement alone that could put me in attack. Probably kill me. What would you want to kill me for, John? For a carpet? You want to kill me for a carpet?"

According to Gacy, he had to quell the situation, soothe Butkovich, who was clearly in a heightened state. The handcuffs once used only a week earlier on Tony were kept in the bar. Switching the whole conversation, Gacy tried to engage Butkovich. He told him about this guy he saw earlier. A cop had him handcuffed and pinned up against the police car. Sulking, Butkovich wasn't interested. But Gacy persisted. "You should have seen it!" He grabbed the cuffs. He wanted to show the boy exactly what had happened.

"Why ya gotta show me?" Butkovich asked.

"Cuz then you'll see. Here." Gacy slipped one of the boy's wrists through the cuffs, instructing him to place his other hand behind his back. He insisted he only needed one second for the trick. That was all it took. With both hands fastened behind his back, the boy couldn't resist. He was utterly helpless.

John later told interviewers; the boy threatened to kill John Gacy once he got out of the handcuffs.

"You just relax," John replied to a heated Butkovich. "I don't take the cuffs off until you sober up. Could take all night." Writhing in a futile effort, the boy tried to free himself, but it was no use. Out of worry for the kid hurting himself, Gacy got him down to the ground, so the boy was on his back. Then Gacy sat upon his chest for a while. He explained it was for the teenager's good.

Again, Gacy claimed, Butkovich threatened him. "When I get these cuffs off, you're a dead man."

"Anyone gets killed, it's you, John. Just sober up, okay?" Gacy responded to the boy.

While waiting for Butkovich to settle down, Gacy returned to the bar and went ahead having several more shots of scotch. Drunk, Gacy got down onto the floor beside Little John. He didn't want to leave the boy alone as he sobered up. He was there to keep him company as the night went by.

That was the last thing Gacy could remember about that night. Butkovich's version of the story will never be known.

Gacy woke up in his bed. He knew he was alone looking around the bedroom, but the drinking had caused his memory to fade. He couldn't remember much about the hours before.

Hunger led him to the kitchen, but a light left on in the living room caught his attention. Had he left it on? It wasn't uncommon for him to pass out in the chair and leave it on. Then his thoughts began to clear a bit more, and he remembered "Little John" Butkovich was over. Gacy figured he'd wake the boy up and make them a good breakfast. He made his way to the living room, but the sight of legs on the floor stopped him.

There was John Butkovich. He was lying in the living room, just as Gacy had left him. Except there was an extra element. A rope was tied tightly around his neck, and the front of his pants was wet like he'd urinated. His skin was now a reddish blue color, but his eyes were shut tightly. Gacy knelt beside him and removed the rope. Pressing his head to his chest, John Gacy listened for a heartbeat. Nothing. No breathing. Just the quiet, still, empty home. He removed the handcuffs. The body hadn't been dead long. It wasn't completely stiff.

John Gacy had no memory of killing him.

He made his way to the garage and grabbed a tarp to roll the body into. But he didn't bury it in the crawl space. Not right away, at least. Instead, he dragged the corpse out to the garage and left it in there for several days—even after Carole returned home. John Butkovich's body stayed out. She was always in the kitchen, blocking his access to the crawl space. John had to improvise soon. The body was deteriorating. He couldn't make it past Carole, but he had an area of soft dirt in the garage where cement hadn't been poured yet. "I took his clothes off, there in the garage so there would be no identification. I thought I should bury him there. So, I dug the hole and put him there, but I had to dig under the foundation because a three-foot hole is not big enough for someone who's five-five or five-six. Whatever. And it was hard to get the hole big enough. So, I had to bend him over, and by this time, he was stiff. I just barely got him in the hole, and I had to jump up and down on him to bend him over and get him deep enough in there," Gacy described later. Then he poured a layer of cement over the makeshift grave.

John Butkovich's car was found abandoned, and when his parents hadn't heard from their son, the police took action. They stopped by Gacy's home to ask about his young employee. Gacy told them that Butkovich had stopped by early one night with friends to fight over some wages. They could ask the friends if they wanted more information; that was all that Gacy recalled.

The police decided Butkovich had run away from home. But the kid's parents knew better. He wouldn't have disappeared without his car or wallet. They called the police, urging them to meet with Gacy once more. They feared for their son's life. And after two years and more than a hundred calls to the station, the police stopped answering the Butkovich's parents' pleas for help. The officers had moved on. The case went cold, and Little John's parents were left without answers on what happened to their child.

It was like this for all Gacy's murders. He remembered little. The Other Guy, what John Wayne Gacy referred to as the dark force that loomed inside of him, took over. It was eviler than Jack Hanley, and when it emerged, his memory disintegrated. Out of the thirty-three murders, Gacy would only be able to recall bits and pieces of them. All else was lost to the Other Guy who inhabited beneath his skin.

When Carole asked about Butkovich, Gacy told her as far as he knew, Little John had run away. Never to be seen again. John Wayne did not offer any further explanation than that.

Pogo the Clown!

Y ou know jackshit! You have no idea how hard I work for you, how hard I work for the girls. Because I want them to have the things they deserve, and you won't help me. You won't work with me. If I had some fucking help around here, I'd have time for you. You're so goddamn dumb; you don't even understand."

"It would be just the same," Carole said, "whatever I did."

"All you ever do is bitch!" John hollered. "Bitch from the time I walk in the door. If I was out banging every other broad in town, you'd have a reason to bitch. If I was gambling away our money, or fucking drinking it up, or buying drugs with it, you'd have reason to bitch. But I'm working! I'm working my ass off seven days a week, twenty fucking hours a day. Where does the money go? All the money goes to you. What do I ever spend on myself? Jesus Christ, Carole, what the fuck do you want from me?"

The divorce came after the disappearance of John Butkovich. Carole had understandably had enough. Their fighting continued, worsening at home. Gacy believed all Carole did was complain and spend money, but he claimed to have not wanted the split to happen. He let her stay in the home through October, even after they divorced in February.

He didn't really want her to leave, but the Other Guy did. The evil man lurking within. That was the one who started fights and made Carole feel dumb, belittling and nitpicking what she did. "The bitch is fucking up a good thing; get rid of her. I want the house to myself." The Other Guy would whisper, breaking through, penetrating his thoughts. The wicked thoughts had always been there, but the dark presence began to emerge more and more after Butkovich.

This did nothing to hinder John's reputation or drive. He worked his way up the Chicago political scene, volunteering for everything, never charging for the work PDM did. It wasn't long until Gacy became an irreplaceable member of the community. Gacy landed a spot as secretary-treasurer of the Norwood Park Township Street Lighting District. And after one year, he moved up to appointed Democratic precinct captain for the Twenty-first Precinct, Norwood Park Township. On foot, Gacy traveled through the neighborhoods for the elections. It wasn't long until the people of Norwood Park knew John and his important political ties.

He was named director of Chicago's annual Polish Constitution Day Parade. A tremendous honor. During his second time in charge of the parade, Gacy made the most out of it politically. He was sure to put all the participating members and politicians in line. He rubbed elbows with essential people and knew how to sell himself. For John, it was the foundation for his future political career.

And in the year of 1975, he grew too old to continue with the Jaycees. In its place, he joined the Moose Lodge. They had a Jolly Joker Clown Club, and

John Wayne Gacy began his work as his most infamous identity, Pogo the Clown. Five or six members of the Jolly Joker Clown Club dressed up as clowns to entertain hundreds of children at holiday parties hosted by the Moose Lodge.

Gacy had his costume custom-made to his liking, designing his own makeup. John became Pogo, visiting hospitals often to sit with the sick children and make them laugh. He even had two puppets made to incorporate into his act. The skunk he carried with him could crack a smile or laugh out of any timid child. Jack Shields, a fellow Chicago clown, thought Gacy was a great clown and excellent with the children. He recalled one of Gacy's acts, "He had a dog leash and a harness he would use. He had a tubing that would run down through the leash to the collar, a bulb in his hand would contain water, and he would caution the children that his invisible dog was just a puppy, and they best be cautious. Like all puppies, sometimes it would wet their shoes, and about the time the child would believe that there was no invisible puppy, he would squeeze the bulb and wet the child's shoes and say, 'Now you excited my little puppy.'" The trick made it look like the puppy peed itself. The children would throw back their heads and squeal with laughter.

For John, donning Pogo the Clown was an escape. He loved making people laugh, but he loved the attention more. Gacy believed becoming a clown gave him a whole new identity. With that identity, he could get away with less acceptable behavior for the average man, especially one aspiring to move up in politics. If he wanted to run up to some woman during a parade and honk her boobs, he could. No one would say anything or tell him otherwise because he was merely a clown. Pogo was trying to get a laugh, not to get a rise sexually.

And when he sat down in front of the mirror and painted the white grease makeup on his face, he took the time to become Pogo, and different events required different versions of Pogo the Clown. The clown who sat in the hospital rooms of sick children was compassionate. Having a lonely childhood, Gacy felt as though he could relate to what these children, who had been lying alone, were going through. He accessed those feelings to portray a tenderhearted friend for the children. As he sat beside them, his goal was to establish trust, and it wasn't long before the young children would begin to smile and laugh, talking to their new clown friend.

If he was the compassionate Pogo at the hospital, then at parties, he became a hatred Pogo for the entitled children at the parties. Notably, the clowns were used to control and monitor the children at these sorts of events, not entertain. John kept watch of the behavior exhibited by the party guests. If he saw the selfish kids reaching for more candy than the others, he made sure to intervene. Gacy didn't mind that his clown smile came to hard, sharp points, scaring some children. That is what the hatred clown was, the one watching greedy children take as much candy as they could muster in their little hands.

They would chase after him, pulling on his costume and lying about not getting any treats. And with every pull, Pogo became a little angrier. More spite built in him. So, when he'd pinch their cheeks, as clowns do, he was sure to squeeze just a bit harder. Leaning forward, beneath the massive blood-red smile, he'd bent down close to the kid's ear to speak in a harsh whisper, "Get your ass away from me, you little motherfucker." He'd laugh and act confused as to why the child now burst into a well of tears.

When Gacy wasn't performing at parties in his clown uniform, he threw them at his own home. He was a social man. His neighbors knew this well. The neighbors took notice of Gacy and how he'd putter late at night around his home. He was up, always moving. There were times past 2 am when the Grexas would see Gacy pull into his driveway accompanied by a group of young men. They didn't think much of it.

Before Gacy began preparations for his Western-themed party, Ed Grexa caught his neighbor in the backyard standing in a hole. It was deep enough to allow a full-grown man to stand inside, and the walls rose to his chest. Curious, Ed walked over and joked with Gacy, asking if the hole was for a grave. Gacy stopped shoveling and looked up at his neighbor hovering over him. "That's an awful thing to say," Gacy responded with a melancholic tone. And just in time for the party, John had installed a permanent barbecue over the massive pit.

Hundreds of people streamed into the home of Summerdale for the party. Gacy's circle of associates had grown and flourished, and he welcomed everyone with his warm and gregarious charm. Even Carole came to help host. The parties were themed, and he was sure to dress up and never drink too much. He'd even dance with the women who had no partner. And when the occasional comment about the musty odor came up, Gacy wrote that off to the flooding in the crawl space.

The party came to an end. Often after one of his events, he would arrive at the Grexas with a platter of beef or ham and make the occasional comment about overdoing it once again for the party. "You got kids," he said, "you can use it."

But when alone and late-night, Gacy began to slip. He started drinking more and more, and then came the pills. Pills to help him fall asleep. Drugs to help him keep calm through the day. Often, he'd have a few strong drinks and sink into his leather chair, then suddenly he'd wake up. Too often, he'd wake up, and he'd find himself driving to New Town, to Clark and Broadway. But that wasn't while he was John Wayne Gacy. On those late nights, he was Jack Hanley.

Twice a week he went down to the park or bus station. If one of the young men caught his eye, John pulled over and talked to them. He figured he was already down there cruising past midnight; he might as well get his "rocks off." He wanted it quick. But he preferred it best at his own home, not in the car parked out at a vacant lot. So, once he lured them in his car, whether it be by force or with the promise of alcohol, Gacy drove them back to Summerdale. He'd wanted them to blow him and "get the fuck away."

Jack Hanley was a part of Gacy the same way Pogo the Clown was. A different branch on the same tree, but instead of making children laugh, Jack Hanley liked clean-cut, well-groomed young boys. He preferred those who were short and well-built with tight asses and lighter hair. He didn't want those who he described as a blatant homosexual. He wanted a young one, inexperienced and naive, who were severely desperate for cash.

If they tried to raise the price on him or outsmart him, Jack was sure to punish them. He'd drop them off somewhere and make them walk back to the park. With some young men he couldn't bring himself to sleep with. Those were boys that were too young or too innocent. Then Jack Hanley became like a father figure, warning the kid he was degrading himself, selling his body for sex, and could end up getting killed. Hustling was no good.

The presence grew. Carole and the girls were no longer around. Nothing held him back. That meant the Other Guy, the one who drove his wife away, appeared more easily and frequently. He was the one who yearned for dark desires.

The Lost Boys

Runaways were not unheard of. A time before social media and cell phones, it was easy to disappear. And for many of the young men that came across Gacy, they too appeared to have simply vanished.

Darrel Sampson was last seen alive on April 6, 1976. Five weeks later, it was May 14th. Randall Reffett vanished. That same day, fourteen-year-old Samuel Stapleton left his sister's house to walk home. It was 11:00 pm, and home was only a block away. Even though it was such a short distance, the boy never made it. Both Reffett and Stapleton were found several years later beneath 8213 Summerdale. It's believed Gacy bound one and made the other watch in horror as he strangled one to death. Their bodies were uncovered in the same grave, buried in a suggestive position.

May 22, 1976, John Wayne Gacy met Michael Rossi while the sixteen-year-old worked on Gacy's kitchen. Rossi initially worked for a plumbing contractor hired by Gacy. John bought a new dishwasher, and Rossi went down into the crawl space to install a new water line. It was dark in the damp, enclosed area. Rossi noticed nothing out of the ordinary. With sandy brown hair and standing at five foot seven, Gacy offered Rossi a job paying far more than the plumber could ever pay him.

John Wayne Gacy conducted the interview first around lunchtime in his own home. During the conversation, Rossi later testified that Gacy mentioned how "liberal" he was about sex. Years later, when the police began their investigation on Gacy, Rossi confessed in a police interview to having an ongoing sexual relationship with Gacy, as it was a term of his employment. He would later deny it in court.

The exact nature of their relations is not entirely clear. John disclosed to authorities that he and Rossi would engage sexually. According to Gacy, Rossi was the first one the handcuff trick worked on. When testifying under oath, Rossi claimed Gacy never put handcuffs on him, nor did they have any sexual relationship. When placed under a lie detector test, it could not be confirmed whether Rossi knew about the murders.

That night after Rossi's job interview, Gacy told during interrogations that he and Rossi met at his home on Summerdale to talk more in-depth about the job. They drank and smoked marijuana. The hazy smoke billowed between them. After a casual chit-chat, Gacy switched the conversation. "What would you do if some guy approached you for sex?" John pried. Standing behind the bar, Rossi answered, "I don't know. It never happened." Gacy fiddled with the handcuffs.

"Hey, I'll show you a trick. You can put these things on and take them off without the key," John offered. According to Gacy, Rossi didn't believe him. So, John told him to snap the metal cuffs on and lock them on his wrist. Rossi did what he was told, and there he stood, now bound, waiting for the grand reveal.

"All right, they're on tight. How do I get 'em off?"

"You don't get 'em off. The trick is you need the key."

Rossi didn't panic. He was a bit unamused by Gacy's trick. "I thought you could slip your hand out or something."

"No way, asshole. And now . . . I'm going to rape you."

Gacy described the events that followed. He stood up, walked over to the teenage boy, stripped him down, sat on his chest, and forced Rossi to perform oral. Then John "got into it orally." Because there was no biting, Gacy believed it was completely consensual. When it was over, Gacy removed the handcuffs, and several more drinks were had. Gacy talked to Rossi about the whole experience; gay sex wasn't as horrible as people made it out to be. They were really helping one another. In his words, John minimized the sexual assault. He told the boy; they were sort of scratching each other's backs.

Late into the night, Gacy drove Rossi home, reminding him that they had work early in the morning. Rossi showed up the next day and continued to work for John Wayne Gacy for the next two years.

William Carroll went missing on June 10. His parents could not find him. Authorities were at a loss. No one could find the boy after that day. That is until authorities searched the crawl space tucked away underneath John's house. He was the twenty-second body removed from Gacy's home. That day, the parents learned the resting place of their child.

Families in the community suffered from the disappearance of their boys. The loss of a child has been known to force a mother's or father's life into a screeching halt, but the day-to-day of others continued.

Gacy, unaffected by the bodies beneath his floor, began preparations for his 'Spirit of 76' party. Over four hundred people attended. John put on a colonial outfit and wore a tricorn hat atop a white wig. A massive 76 had been mowed into the front lawn. Politicians pooled in, and all the neighbors were invited. The guests drank from the kegs of beer and listened to the music from the small band he hired to play. They laughed and enjoyed themselves. For those attending, everything was normal.

Guests danced, laughed, and joked. All of them unaware of the bodies beneath their feet, silent and still. Young men stashed away. Snatched from their families and left to rot underneath the joyful footsteps of John Wayne Gacy's guests.

The more time passed, the more confident John Wayne Gacy grew. After Rossi, Gacy realized that his handcuff trick worked reasonably well. He became a little cocky about his sly tricks. He believed, "You'd have to be pretty dumb and stupid to let a stranger put you in a pair of handcuffs."

But on the night of July 26, 1976, Gacy learned this trick was not infallible. Eighteen-year-old David Cram walked along the roadside with his thumb up, intending to hitchhike. A man pulled up beside him in an Oldsmobile. PDM contracting signs stuck in the car's windows. Cram hopped into the stranger's vehicle upon invitation. The two began to talk about work. Cram shared that he currently held a job at a tire repair shop. Naturally, Gacy inquired about Cram's paycheck. Gacy offered him a job with more pay and told Cram if he was serious he should give Gacy a call later. John gave his number, and the two continued on their drive.

Cram made the call that very night, and Gacy had several employees pick him up to bring him to the Summerdale house. David Cram noticed they were all teenage boys. The young employees had an urgent job to take care of and left the Summerdale house. The teenagers drove in a truck together, except Cram, who rode in the Oldsmobile alone with Gacy.

His new employer quickly began to talk himself up about the college degrees he had. One in sociology and the other in psychology, which he stressed to Cram was an important degree. It helped with manipulating people.

The conversation seemed to shift. His new employer's words began to string together and become muddled. He started speaking about how an employee might move up in PDM then slipping in that he is bisexual. Cram listened and began to understand the underlying message. Gacy was implying those who scratched each other's backs had the opportunity to make more. Then Gacy switched the conversation back to the type of work to expect at PDM. The "image he painted for me, was like, bulldozers and cranes, you know, tall sky-scrapers and that's what I thought we'd be doing," Cram later recounted, but in reality, they were on their way to paint Oppie's hot dog stand. Not as glamorous as working in the big city.

The next few weeks passed. Cram continued his work for PDM. He spent one day cleaning out Gacy's garage. He came across several wallets. Curiosity overcame his politeness. He opened them and found several identifications of young men. One matched his description well, even looked like him. Cram figured he could use it to buy liquor since he was underage. He asked Gacy if he could keep it to use. According to Cram, Gacy "just chuckled it off and said that I didn't want those, those were from some deceased person or something like that, something that had to do with some kind of syndicate." He had told his young employee that he also worked in the syndicate who set up hits on people. Strange thing to learn about your boss, but Cram didn't seem to give it much thought. He probably saw Gacy as an eccentric person in the first place who stretched stories or elaborated them for dramatic effect.

The idea that John Wayne Gacy was a hitman may have been born out of a need to brag about getting away with murder. It's a terrible secret to keep all to oneself, and he continued to kill teenagers seemingly without repercussions. A twisted person like Gacy may have wanted to revel his disturbing habits, giddy at the idea he was not caught. He could continue pursuing his dark desires, killing boys and young men without much notice.

Rick Johnston was no different from the other lost teens. In August, the eighteen-year-old left his home to enjoy some music at the concert. Sadly, for the teenager and his parents, he never returned home from the show. His family wept the sudden absence of their boy only to find him later, as the twenty-third body removed from Summerdale. Another victim of the deranged killer.

John Wayne Gacy may have tried to share his perverted habits in a way he thought was sly. It seemed others, not just Cram, saw Gacy's stories as an exaggeration. He was known to brag and flourish. David Cram must not have worried too much about the syndicate, hitman work because toward the end of August, only a few weeks after Gacy killed Rick Johnston, Gacy offered Cram a room at Summerdale. August 21, 1976, David Cram moved into the three-bedroom house.

The day it was his nineteenth birthday, he was out with some friends drinking and partying. It was late into the night when Cram returned home. He was already drunk. He probably stumbled slightly upon entering the house. When he opened the door, he found Gacy dressed in his full Pogo uniform. His pale white face and sharp-pointed smile. David Cram may have given John a look of confusion or discomfort. Gacy explained to Cram he had a charity event the next day and was preparing. He figured to celebrate Cram's birthday, he'd leave the makeup and costume on for him.

They moved to the bar area behind the living room. Cram was already drunk, but the jolly clown went ahead and poured several hefty shots of the strong stuff. Gacy went ahead and took a few tranquilizers. He'd been taking a lot of valium lately. Strung out on weed, tranquilizers, and booze, Gacy began to perform in his clown suit. Cram described the scene, "[Gacy] was showing me some of his puppets and so on and so on. Then he came up with a handcuff trick, how you can escape from handcuffs. He demonstrated them, and he shook them off. I was so plowed; I didn't, you know, really pay attention to it."

After a bit more urging, Cram willingly held out his wrists to Pogo the Clown, who slapped the cold metal. It tightened around his wrists, and Gacy revealed the punch line. The way out was with the key. The killer was probably so self-satisfied to see the trick worked again so neatly.

Cram wanted the cuffs removed immediately, but instead, Gacy grabbed hold of him and swung him around. Cram's voice turned into pleads and shouts. Then the atmosphere changed. The jolly Pogo morphed into something evil. The warm clown smile on Pogo's face became vile and sinister, twisting into sharp points. "I'm going to rape you," Gacy said in a menacing voice. His hands released their grip. Cram staggered back to the tv stand, but he remained steady on his feet. Pogo was confident. He had his next victim and moved slowly toward Cram, savoring each moment. His prey was completely under his control. Nowhere for him to escape.

At least, that is what Gacy thought. Unbeknownst to Pogo, Cram had spent a year in the army. He was trained for combat; the teenager knew how to fight. The young man used that knowledge to his advantage. Cram lurched forward, kicking Gacy hard against his head. With a solid thud, the clown fell to the floor, with a thud, giving Cram enough time to get the keys and free himself.

They stared at one another in silence. No words were spoken, just the hum of the house in the late hours of the night. Cram walked away from the living room and locked himself in his bedroom, leaving the beaten clown alone.

He lived there for one more month. Gacy would come into his room at night in those four weeks and try to sleep with Cram. In the act of self-defense, Cram wore an old pair of jeans to bed because he learned it slowed Gacy down. The process of his boss trying to undo his jeans woke Cram up. Once alert, he could stop it from going any further.

On David Cram's last night in Summerdale, his eyes snapped open. It wasn't what he saw that was the most frightening; it was what he heard. From across the hall in his bedroom, Gacy called out to David in a singsong, high-pitched voice, "Dave, you know what I want." He sang through the house. John made sure that his roommate could hear his wicked words. Cram chose to ignore it, lying in the bedroom, but Gacy refused to be overlooked that night. He barged into Cram's room, lunged onto the bed, pushing his forearm against Cram's throat. David Cram shoved him off, and the two began to grapple and fight until Cram pinned Gacy beneath him. David brought his arm up, raised to strike. Gacy appeared to have lost consciousness then, and Cram lowered his arm. Cram later described how Gacy came to, left the bedroom, turned in the doorway, and said, "You ain't no fun," before going back to bed. Cram moved out the next day and quit PDM to start his own contracting business.

With his house now empty again, Gacy invited Michael Rossi to move in. Rossi agreed and started paying rent. The way John saw it, he was sort of taking in stray animals and giving them a home.

Rossi took well to the work. He quickly became Gacy's right-hand man, and Gacy promoted him to a supervisor position. And although Rossi testified to have never slept with his employer, Gacy said otherwise. He claimed they had sex whenever Gacy wanted it. According to John, there was no kissing or love. It was about dominating Rossi. "Get on it, Rossi!" he would say if Rossi wanted something or to use the truck for dates. Gacy described how Rossi would tease him and get him all worked up to make demands before finishing. Carole, who visited on occasion, noticed how they manipulated one another. John later told her that Rossi was like a son to him.

Rossi remained high up in Gacy's employee list, but John always needed more laborers. As usual, he sought out teenagers to fill his quota. Gregory Godzik was seventeen years old during the winter of 1976. He was charming with bright gray eyes and dark blonde hair, standing around five foot nine, he was lean and trim. He had no problem scoring a date with one of the girls at Taft High School, and he was well-liked, always out hanging with friends. Landing a job at PDM was what he described as the best job he's ever had. Gacy offered him twice the salary of what he made at the Republic Lumber Company.

The year 1976 was quickly turning into one of the greatest of Godzik's life. December 11th, he told his mom he'd finally scored a date with a pretty sophomore he had fought another boy over. He put on a brand-new shirt he'd bought himself. His sister recalled that night and how Greg "...was just very, very concerned on how he looked. He had on new pants, new shoes, and a new shirt. He was very excited about going out." Around 12:30 am when he dropped his date off at her home in his old car; he worked tirelessly to fix it up. He promised to call her later.

But Greg never called his date. He never made it back home that night.

What Gacy remembered was broken and hazy. He vaguely remembered picking Greg up to buy some pot from the high schooler. They went to his house, and according to Gacy, an argument about weed and money started. It was hard for John to recall much, but what he did remember clearly was waking up Sunday morning, and there was Gregory Godzik dead in the living room. The handcuffs around his wrist, arms behind his back, a rope tied tightly around his neck. He was in nothing but his underwear. Gacy dumped his body into the crawl space, burying him deep beneath the house's foundation, Gregory still and stiff in the sitting position.

When Gregory's mother awoke, she went into her son's bedroom to find the bed empty. She phoned several of his friends. No one had answers. It wasn't like Greg to stay away from home, and if he had unexpected plans, he was always sure to call his parents and let them know. But they heard nothing. And when they went to the police, they were told their son was most likely a runaway. The Godziks refused to believe it.

The Sunday after Greg's date, the police came upon the teenager's maroon 1966 Pontiac, unlocked and abandoned, sitting in the back parking lot of a pet store. The Godziks knew their son treasured his car, how he'd spent tireless hours keeping it running.

She phoned her son's employer, who told her that Gregory had called him several days before he disappeared and left a message on his voicemail. The message was Greg saying he'd come into work the next day. She asked for the tape, but Gacy couldn't show it to her. It had already been conveniently erased. Mrs. Godzik told the police about her conversation with Gacy, but there was nothing on his record. Marco Butkovich was calling law enforcement during this time, begging them to speak with John Gacy about his missing son. But the parents were communicating with two different police departments, and there was no communication between the two.

The calendar read January 20, 1977. As Gacy recalled, it was raining that night as he cruised in his Oldsmobile. Bits of the story were broken, but this came as no surprise. Gacy struggled to remember parts of the night as he did with almost all his victims. Through the droplets streaking down his windshield, he spotted a kid walking down the street. John couldn't resist. He pulled over to speak with him.

The teenager introduced himself as John Szyc. According to John, they struck up a conversation, and Szyc mentioned wanting to sell his car to leave town. Gacy expressed interest in buying the car. He asked if Szyc had the title on him; he did. So, they agreed to go back to Gacy's house and talk it over.

The young man might have been excited at his luck for finding a buyer so quickly. John Wayne Gacy probably felt the same way but for a vastly different reason. The two may have chatted casually in the car.

They ended up back at the house. Drinks were involved. Maybe drugs, it was hard for Gacy to recall. He remembered there being three people in the house; most everything else was foggy. Whatever occurred that night was gone to him; the next morning at seven-thirty, John Gacy woke up. He had experienced another blackout episode. That morning Michael Rossi was home, asleep on the couch in the front room, and John Szyc was dead on the other bedroom's floor. Unsure if

Rossi knew about the dead boy, Gacy got out of bed quietly and tip-toed to the bedroom. He collected Szyc's body, tossing it down into the crawl space.

Rossi found the title of Szyc's car, a white 1971 Plymouth Satellite. The paper was left out on the bar, and he brought it up to Gacy. They went together to retrieve it. Rossi drove the Plymouth back to Summerdale, and after the drive, he told Gacy he was confident he wanted the car now. They argued over the value. The two arrived at six hundred dollars. Rossi didn't have the whole amount on him yet, but he paid Gacy $300 and promised to pay the rest of it off over time. When the police later found the title, it was noted how Szyc's name on the title looked nothing like his signature.

The first victim recovered from John Wayne Gacy's crawl space was the twenty-year-old Jon Prestige from Kalamazoo, Michigan. He was last seen on March 15, 1977. The young man intended to explore Bughouse Square, also known as Chicago's Washington Square Park. He probably was interested in attending one of the many free-speech gatherings. Regardless of the reason for his visit, after listening to a lecture from a soapbox, John Prestige disappeared.

One month after Prestige's untimely disappearance, John decided to have Rossi move out. His excuse for the sudden change of heart was he didn't want anyone to get the wrong idea about a young man living alone with an older male. That is at least what he told Rossi. Taking the news rather well, Rossi found himself his own apartment.

Shortly after he left, Doreen, the woman Gacy had been dating off and on, moved in. It was overall viewed as a happy relationship. They had a "sexual relationship," but it was disclosed that Gacy couldn't manage to have an erection. Doreen had colostomy surgery done, and Gacy blamed his erectile dysfunction on the operation. He claimed when moments became heated, and her clothes came off, he lost interest. He also thought she read too many "women's lib" books. In John's opinion, Doreen wanted too much and never did anything around the house. She never wanted to cook or clean because of all the ideas she read in her feminist books.

It was easy to say they were not a perfect match. Their living arrangements ended only after a few months together. In early July, Doreen moved out of Summerdale. Gacy once again had the house to himself. It seems he knew exactly how he wanted to celebrate his newfound freedom. The day after celebrating America's Independence Day, Matthew Bowman went missing only to be found years later beneath Gacy's home.

In August, Gacy had Rossi head down into the crawl space to dig a trench line. To PDM employees, it did not seem out of the ordinary. John Wayne Gacy routinely asked his employees to do work around his home. He and several other employees headed down to the musty, dark pit to shovel according to their boss's exact specifications. And Gacy was particular about where to dig. If anyone went outside the designated area, their boss became angry and started hollering, letting them know they'd messed up.

The work was completed to Gacy's orders, and the young men were none the wiser. September came. Autumn began. In Illinois, that meant the leaves changed colors. From green to red, orange, yellow, the Midwestern greenery transformed. September 15th, shortly after the fresh trenches had been dug up, Robert Gilroy disappeared. The young man, eighteen years old, was known by friends and family as one who loved nature. He was known to spend much of his time outside or with his favorite animal, horses. Gilroy began a typical journey, hitchhiking his way to the Blue Ribbon Stables. To his parents' horror, he never returned.

Only ten days later, another teenage boy went missing. John Mowery, nineteen and an ex-marine, was gone. It wasn't until October 17th that John Mowery's loved ones discovered he never came back from a disco at Clark and Broadway. He was later located with the other young men. Young men who Gacy could never recall how their bodies appeared beneath his floorboards.

The mysterious disappearances continued. The weather began to get colder; leaves drifted from the trees and blanketed the ground. Autumn was in full swing. November 11, Robert Winch went missing. No one had any leads to his whereabouts.

Exactly one week later, Tommy Baling visited a bar on the north side separate from his betrothed. The young man may have needed one night out by himself. He spent his evening watching *Bonnie and Clyde.* The night began innocently but turned dark and foreboding. Baling never returned home; there was no evidence as to where he went. It wasn't until his fiancé identified his body after it was pulled from Gacy's home that the young man was found. His poor fiancé was able to confirm her departed love's identity by the wedding ring on his finger.

Shortly after Baling, nineteen-year-old David Talsma had a night planned for himself. He scored tickets to a rock concert. His day may have begun with a lot of excitement; he could have bragged to all his friends about his plans. Plans that went astray. That night, Talsma never came back, claimed as another plaything to satisfy John Wayne Gacy's desires.

All these faces, all the young men. The body count grew and grew. One might think each encounter would be memorable, but when the doctors showed Gacy photos of these victims, he only remembered one person. He could only recognize John Szyc's face. The rest were simply casualties of his unquenchable cruelty.

Gacy started using Preludin, up to seventy milligrams a day, to help counteract all the Valium he needed to relax. The Valium slowed the world down, a little too much. John could not live a relaxed lifestyle. There was far too much work to be done. During the day, the focus and energy from Preludin made him more efficient. But with all the stimulation, Gacy had to take even more Valium to calm back down at night. When that did not seem to be enough, he'd smoke more marijuana and drink. He'd come home from work, hopped up on Preludin, take a few Valium, down half a bottle of scotch, smoke, have a few sleeping pills, and then he'd wake up in the middle of the night, cruising.

December 31st was a cold night in Chicago. Nineteen-year-old Robert Donnelly was out walking through the windy city. He was the oldest of eight children, and after the recent death of his father, he became responsible for taking care of his family. The walk may not have been for leisure but rather to help cope with the newfound burden he carried. He was in therapy to help cope with the stress, and he was a slow talker with a stutter. He did not have an easy road ahead.

Gacy was out driving along the same street Donnelly strolled. The clock showed it was after midnight. The moon was high. He stopped the car right beside the teenager. He whipped out a gun, impersonating a police officer, and demanded Donnelly get in the black Oldsmobile. Scared and confused, Donnelly obeyed, only to be immediately handcuffed. Gacy sped home with the handcuffed boy, his prisoner.

John Wayne Gacy did not attempt to keep up the façade that he was an officer arresting a potential prostitute. There was no talk about money or sex on the car ride to Gacy's house. It didn't matter if Donnelly wasn't a sex worker nor if he was gay. That would not change the manic murderer's intentions.

There in Gacy's Summerdale home, he threw a drink on the scared boy. Some speculate it was to encourage the victim to remove their clothing. Another drink was poured down his throat. Overcome with crazed lust, he raped Donnelly in several painful ways. At one point, he tied something tightly around his throat and choked him.

There was a moment where Gacy pulled out the gun once again, aiming the barrel directly at Donnelly. It was time to play Russian Roulette. He told him that one of the chambers was loaded. He pulled the trigger twelve times until a blank shot out with a loud bang. Gacy set down the gun and wrapped his massive hands tightly around Donnelly's throat, suffocating the young man until he passed out.

Robert Donnelly came to with his hands still handcuffed and something shoved down his throat, gagging him. Gacy dunked his head beneath the bathwater, over and over. Waterboarding. Choking and suffocating Donnelly. He kept him on the brink of death. The pain and agony were immense. Donnelly begged Gacy to kill him to end the living nightmare. Maybe this is what the murderer wanted to hear all along. He abused, molested, and tormented the teenager until his sick desires felt temporarily satiated.

Within the first week of January, only about a week after Donnelly's night of torture, Chicago police officer Ted Janus pulled up to 8213 Summerdale. The home of John Wayne Gacy. He matched the plate numbers on the Oldsmobile sitting in the driveway. Out walked Gacy, who started to get into his car. He may or may not have noticed the police vehicle in front of his house. To make sure he didn't drive away, Janus quickly put his car in gear and blocked Gacy in.

John Wayne Gacy was under arrest for kidnapping and deviate sexual assault.

Gacy acted astounded as he was instructed to place his hands onto his car's dashboard. He knew nothing about any kidnapping or sexual assault. He calmly invited Janus inside to talk about things over a drink. Instead, he was brought to the Area 6 police station. Inside the interview room, Gacy insisted he didn't need a lawyer. He was willing to be questioned and give answers to whatever they needed. He was innocent.

Gacy told the investigators about December 31st, which was far different from the one Robert Donnelly had come forward with. Gacy saw the boy walking down Montrose Avenue late that night and offered him a ride. They started chatting and agreed on a sexual bargain. Gacy explained it as sex slavery. Donnelly and Gacy returned to Summerdale, where they bound one another in chains and handcuffs and fooled around, taking turns pleasuring one another. There was no payment, and Gacy even drove the kid to work the next morning.

Donnelly's slow manner of speaking and stutter couldn't compare to the gregarious, charming Gacy.

The assistant state's attorney Jerry Latherow believed Gacy was a far better witness. Donnelly was stressed, shaken still from the death of his father. How could that young man compare to John Wayne Gacy? Gacy was a well-respected business owner and an essential part of the community's political scene. Using his excellent people skills worked out once again for the murderer. His public reputation saved his story, gave him the benefit of the doubt.

With the turn of the new year, Gacy started to see Carole again. Doreen was gone; he needed a new female partner. And he had plans. Plans to sell PDM and move somewhere with Carole and the girls far away from the big city. Away from any temptation of the Other Guy who lurked beneath his skin in the shadows of his mind. If there were no hustlers, then there was no reason for Hanley to come out.

But the Other Guy wouldn't have any of it. They had a good thing going for them. And in the spring of '78, there would be no turning back. No option of moving somewhere south to slow down.

A month after Gacy's initial arrest, William Kindred vanished in Chicago's north side. The nineteen-year-old was last seen on February 16th and three months prior, he'd proposed to Mary Jo Paulus and planned to marry her as soon as he got a new job. The two were young and in love, more than excited to start their lives together.

That night in February, he left her apartment with plans to go out to the bars. But he never came back to Mary Jo's. She spent weeks driving around, asking if anyone knew what happened to her young fiancé. She posted his information on wanted posters throughout the city. Mary Jo worked to find her lost love but to no avail. No one had any information or answers until the next year when police asked her to come to the station to identify some clothing and jewelry articles. Those were the last identifiable pieces of the tenth body exhumed from 8213 Summerdale.

The Unheard Witness

Twenty-six-year-old Jeff Rignall left his girlfriend's apartment after an argument over their relationship. He decided to step out for a drink and cool off. It was a cold spring night at the end of March. As he began walking, a black Oldsmobile with antennas sticking out and bright spotlights pulled up beside him.

Gacy's car window was already rolled down. He leaned forward, peering up at Rignall, and asked him, "Hey, where did you get such a good tan?" Rignall told him he had recently been down in Florida. When Gacy asked where he was headed, Rignall gave him the name of one of the local bars—one popular with the gay community. With a joint in hand, Gacy took a hit and offered to give the young man a ride. As Rignall slid into the front seat, he took note of the custom license plate with the three letters PDM and two numbers.

Rignall pegged Gacy as one of the older guys uncomfortable with their sexuality who prowled late at night to find sex, hiding it from his wife and kids. Gacy carried on a conversation about his place down in Florida as the joint moved between them. Rignall turned to take the joint for his second hit as they neared the bar when he was hit with a wet cloth. "It had a cold feeling to it," Rignall recalled, "and I immediately started having like a buzzing-bee sensation in my head, and I went unconscious."

His head now swimming through a fog, Rignall stirred awake. Strapped down to his car seat, all he could do was watch the passing headlights. One after the other. Yellow to red. Red to yellow. Gacy must have noticed his regained consciousness because he pressed the rag against Rignall's mouth again. Blackness. He stirred awake once more, and this time he saw the exit sign for Cumberland off the highway before Gacy's thick hands pressed the rag hard against his face.

In bits and fragments, Rignall remembered the night; how he was lifted and carried by Gacy into the Summerdale home. He felt like a ragdoll the way he was being tossed around. The cold, wet cloth pushed against his face. The darkness returned, and when he gained consciousness, he found himself on a couch. A bar top came into view, and above it was the painting of a sad clown. Gacy stood behind the bar, making himself a drink. Rignall asked, "Why did you do that to me?"

Gacy's voice was harsh as he spoke. "There is a gun under the bar, and I'd just as soon kill you as look at you." In the light of the living room, Rignall saw the form of Gacy; the overweight man remained calm, smoking another joint. He offered a hit to Rignall, who refused. Again, Gacy covered Rignall's face with the chloroform.

A hard hand slapped Rignall. The impact returned him to the nightmare. He looked down to find he had been stripped down naked and restrained. His head and arms were locked into a wooden board attached to the ceiling with chains, and another device bound his feet. Standing in front of Rignall was Gacy, naked and masturbating. Gacy told Rignall how he was now in control of the young man, and Gacy would do whatever he wanted, how he wanted. Between them were a variety of instruments—some leather whips, others metal-like fireplace tools, along with plastic and rubber dildos. Gacy forced Rignall to perform oral, and during it, he demanded Rignall repeat, "I love it. I love it."

Again, the rag clasped over Rignall's face. The chloroform began to burn his skin. This time when Rignall came to, Gacy picked up one of the tools on the floor. Rignall described how Gacy "picked up one of the instruments, told me what he was going to do with it, and started injecting it until I showed physical pain." Rignall did his best to resist screaming or shouting, worried his pain might excite the man further.

"You love it," Gacy said with scorn. "I want to hear you say you love it." Another one of Gacy's tools was shoved into Rignall. Then another douse of chloroform.

Returning to consciousness, Rignall felt Gacy's head resting on his shoulder, inserting something anally. Rignall assumed it was Gacy himself. And what more surprising was someone knelt in front of Rignall on his knees. Brown hair parted in the middle, and when the one in the front noticed Rignall had woken, he was immediately put out again.

In the cold, wet snow beneath a statue of Alexander Hamilton, Rignall woke up from the nightmare. His face was raw and burning from the chloroform. He returned to his girlfriend's apartment, bloodied and beaten after surviving a night of Gacy's horrors. He immediately made a report with the police and spent three weeks at Grant Hospital. He later found out the chloroform severely damaged his liver. There was nothing the law could do with the information Rignall provided. There were hundreds of thousands of black cars in Chicago.

But Rignall refused to accept defeat. He wanted revenge. With two friends, Rignall rented a car and waited by the Cumberland exit for the black Oldsmobile.

Finally, they spotted Gacy cruising along in late April. They followed him to 8213 Summerdale. Rignall sent the address and license plate number to his attorney. At the police station in Area 6, where Robert Donnelly had gone, Rignall was informed about Gacy's past sexual conviction in Iowa. The police agreed to obtain Gacy's mug shot for Rignall.

Rignall called the station daily. "At that time," he later said, "they asked me if I was gay. I was honest with them. I said, 'Yes.' From that point on, I got no cooperation at all." But he was determined not to give up. It took around three weeks, but he finally was granted access to several mug shot books. He identified Gacy immediately. He met with an officer and an assistant state's attorney. They had a hard time believing his story. "When I started getting into the physical aspect of what the man had done to me," Rignall remembered, "they began to make me believe *I* was the crazy one, that he was quote-unquote a model citizen." Rignall was told if he wanted to pursue Gacy, then he would need to issue a civil assault warrant. The police were not going to charge him.

In early May, Gacy had been spending time with Carole and the two girls. He claimed later to have had no memory of Rignall. The whole story was ridiculous to him. The police had found chloroform, but it could be explained—contractors use it as a solvent. And he figured it was far too risky to have a man drugged in the passenger seat if he had gotten pulled over. Plus, the second guy with brown hair parted down the middle, a lot of men wear their hair that way, including Rossi. Gacy admitted sometimes there was three-way sex with his employees and a pickup, but that was all consensual. John never used a gun, let alone drive with drugs in his car. He claimed to have absolutely no recollection of such a night. He figured it never happened, and Rignall was nothing more than a disgruntled hustler looking for payment.

No guilt or fear about Rignall bothered Gacy, as he, Carole, and the girls drove up to Wisconsin to enjoy the warm spring. Like a family once again. They returned home around nine. Carole described the night. "John and I had both, I think we were looking very forward to the time again to be together, and we started, tried to start to make love. And John broke down and cried. He couldn't do anything, and he said it didn't have anything to do with me, that he waited for this, for the day for me to be back in bed with him. And he said he was afraid he was going the other way." They didn't speak as John continued weeping; all Carole could do was hold him until he settled down, and then the two of them went to bed.

O'Rourke, standing at five foot nine and one hundred fifty pounds, had recently met a contractor on the Northwest side who promised good work. He told his roommates he was heading to grab some cigarettes in mid-June, never to return. He was the first body identified that was discovered floating in the Des Plaines River. He was one of the last four thrown over the bridge on Interstate 55.

His murdering spree continued, Gacy began preparations for one of the most important parades of his life—the Polish Constitution Day Parade.

He managed a greater number of moving parts, more than any other parade in his career. There were over fifty floats and twenty bands to operate. Important influences would be there. Rosalynn Carter, the President's wife, was making the appearance as the special guest of honor. He worked with the secret service, planning out the proper protocol. Somehow Gacy managed to pass the secret service background check and receive official clearance. And later in the evening, at the private reception, Rosalynn Carter stood beside Gacy and they snapped a photo together.

On May 7, 1978, Rignall's attorney wrote Gacy a letter, informing him that Jeff Rignall had issued a warrant for Gacy's arrest. But Rignall could not get the police to serve his civil arrest warrant. He called them daily, but they were completely neglecting his requests.

For two months, they ignored him. Frustrated but undeterred, Rignall refused to give up. Fed up, he drove to Gacy's home at 8213 Summerdale on July 15th. A woman answered the door with her hair freshly dyed and makeup done up. She invited Rignall in, introducing herself as John's mother. She was in town for her annual visit. She answered the door pleasantly and informed Rignall that Gacy was out getting the dog groomed. She asked if Rignall was attending Gacy's party that evening.

"I don't know if your son told you," Rignall said, "but there's a warrant out for his arrest." The woman didn't want to hear any of it. She informed him he could swing by later to speak with Gacy if he wanted, but Rignall wanted her to know the truth about her son. He asked if she knew about Gacy's sex crime conviction back in Iowa. Gacy's mother's face became cold and stern. Her white skin became almost as red as the lipstick she had on. She slammed the door quickly after telling Rignall they no longer speak of that.

Rignall turned away, but he saw the PDM van come around the corner. He called the police. This time they arrived, but there was no Gacy. Instead, they found a teenager with brown hair parted down the middle. He approached Rignall and asked if he would kindly please not bring up the rape with John's mother.

In response, John decided to file a countercomplaint against Rignall and claimed Rignall had shoved him and pushed the sexually stimulating drug, known as Rush, in his face.

The day the case was called, Rignall appeared, but Gacy did not. Instead, Michael Rossi arrived in his place, letting the court know Gacy was down in Florida on business. If Gacy had arrived, both the complaints would have most likely been dropped. But Gacy hadn't appeared, and Rignall's lawyer was able to have Gacy's complaint dropped, and the warrant reissued.

Gacy then offered to settle the matter outside of court and pay Rignall three thousand dollars. It was what Rignall's lawyer figured would be the best-case scenario for them. It came nowhere near Rignall's hospital bills. Those added up to twenty-five thousand dollars.

During the summer of 1978, the neighbors directly across the street had a large dog named Susie. She barked often, but one night her deep, loud barks were constant, almost hysterical. Something was wrong. Peering through the back window, they could see the light above Gacy's garage, lighting the yard. Susie continued to bark, straining, hollering. Then they saw a young man struggling to walk between the house and garage, falling into the shrubs. The dog hurriedly pawed at the door. The neighbor stepped outside onto their lawn. All they heard were haggard, strained breaths rising and falling. They phoned the police, but nothing was found. At times, screams would wake them late in the night, but it was impossible to know from where. Other neighbors lived closer; they'd be able to call the police. But the screams never stopped, only faded away.

The evening of July 15th, after Rignall left Gacy's now flustered mother, the party continued at 8213

Summerdale. It was Gacy's fifth annual party. This year the theme was the Italian Festival. Hundreds of people pooled into the home like they did every year. Gacy wore a peasant's costume to piss off his wealthy friends. Business was increasing, and '78 was PDM's best year. He ran around the city and to other states, working on job sites. Most of which were pharmacies where Gacy had full access to the drugs behind the counter.

During this time, John claimed he wore himself down working too hard. No boys died for five months at his hand, but all of that changed when Carole announced she was getting remarried.

The calendar read November 4. Frank Landingin, released from prison the day before, met with his father at a bar. Nineteen years old, he was a tough kid from the streets, hustled drugs. He left the bar with the intention to find his girlfriend and hopefully make amends. He was last seen around three o'clock in the morning walking just off Broadway. His body was found eight days later floating down the Des Plaines

River. His underwear was shoved down his throat, gagging him. Twelve of Gacy's victims died from choking on cloth-like material in their throat, but the autopsy revealed he died from choking on his vomit.

Three weeks after Landingin, James "MoJo" Mazzara was discovered in the Des Plaines River. He had just returned to Chicago after a Thanksgiving holiday with his family. He was last seen walking alone toward Bughouse Square with a suitcase in hand.

Hired to Die

The Des Plaines River was a focal point for a young Eagle Scout. Fifteen-year-old Robert Piest was only two merit badges away from becoming an Eagle Scout. A good student and sophomore at Maine West High School, he loved the outdoors and planned to get the highest merit badge with a community service project of cleaning up the river. He was well built and a member of the high school gymnastics team. He dated girls a year or two older than him. With brown, shaggy hair and an athletic build, he was precisely Gacy's type.

He was three weeks away from turning sixteen, and he had big plans to save up for a Jeep. Working for $2.30 an hour at the Nisson Pharmacy wasn't quite enough for the car of his dreams. He needed a higher paying job.

On December 11th, around 5:00 pm, Elizabeth Piest picked up her son from gymnastics practice. Usually, there was no time for dinner together, but he finished early, so they had enough time for a quick meal at home. Tonight was Elizabeth's forty-sixth birthday. The family was going to celebrate with cake and ice cream later in the evening around nine when Robert's shift at Nisson ended.

At 5:30, John Wayne Gacy strolled into Nisson Pharmacy. The owner called him in to do some minor work. Gacy walked around, took measurements, and discussed plans with the pharmacy owner for an hour. He wanted sixteen hundred dollars for the job. The pharmacist figured he could do the work himself and just wanted some of Gacy's advice. It was about 6:00 in the evening when Rob showed up. He marked prices on inventory and stocked shelves. Immediately, Gacy's gaze fell upon him.

"Looks like you got a new crew," Gacy said while watching Piest. "A lot of new faces." The pharmacist mentioned that most of his workers are young men who eventually move on to full-time jobs or college.

"I've been hiring a lot of high school boys to work for me," Gacy responded.

In front of Piest, Gacy continued talking with one of the other workers. A woman named Linda Mertes. She remembered Gacy from previous work he had done at the pharmacy. She asked about how Rossi was doing. Within Piest's earshot, Gacy was not shy to mention how well Rossi was doing and how well paid he was. His employees earned around seven dollars an hour. About triple what Piest got at Nisson Pharmacy.

Gacy claimed he never offered a job to Piest. They never spoke. Instead, it was around seven when Gacy left. The owner of the pharmacy found Gacy's appointment book sitting behind the counter. It appeared Gacy had forgotten it.

PDM's business owner had a seven o'clock business meeting with Richard Rapheal, but he didn't show. Gacy was known for his punctuality. He never missed meetings. But this time, he did. It was unlike him. Rapheal reached out to get an answer, but there was no response. Every time he called, it went straight to Gacy's answering machine.

In Gacy's version, he headed home to switch vehicles for plowing. Fresh, white snow fell over Chicago that evening and collected on the ground and roads. Upon running home, he noticed the pharmacist left a message about leaving his appointment book on the counter. Contradicting John Wayne Gacy's story, according to the owner of Nisson, he never called Gacy that evening.

"Nisson Drugs is on the way to Glenview," John explained. "I figured I could pick up my book, then drive out to Glenview for my meeting." That was why he swung by a second time. Robert Piest had nothing to do with the visit.

Around 7:30 pm, seventeen-year-old Kim Byers stood behind the cash register at Nisson. She noticed Piest had draped his blue Pacific Trails parka over the counter. Being close to the door, every time a customer walked in and out of the store, a hard blast of the cold winter air whipped in. She grabbed Robert Piest's jacket and slipped it on. At this time, business slowed down. Kim pulled some negatives of photos taken from the homecoming dance. She wanted to get them printed and enlarged for Christmas gifts. Tearing the top receipt off the photo, number 36119, she tucked it into the parka's pocket, forgetting it belonged to Piest. Then she got the negatives ready to be dropped off and developed.

A little after eight, Gacy pulled up to Nisson Pharmacy to get his appointment book back. Even though he was now late for his meeting, he took time measuring out the pharmacy, walking around. He figured he could strike a deal, figure out ways to save money for the modifications. He headed to the back, where the door was opened. There was Robert Piest, folding boxes. Gacy swore he asked Piest if the kid knew anything about shelving. That was it—all the conversation they had.

Around eight-forty, Gacy headed back to his black truck with the plow on the front end. He said he got in and began writing down figures even though he was well over an hour late for the meeting. At 8:50 pm, Robert's mother arrived to pick up her son. She was ten minutes early and wasted time perusing the store's stocked shelves. With a few minutes left before close, Rob asked Kim if she would take over the register so he could speak with the contractor guy outside in his truck. He put on his blue parka and stepped out into the cold winter. Kim forgot about the photo receipt she'd slipped into its pocket earlier. On his way out, Rob found his mother. She probably was excited to get back home and celebrate her birthday with her family.

"Mom, wait a minute," he said. "I've got to talk to a contractor about a summer job that will pay me five dollars an hour." She agreed.

The rest of the night is only known from Gacy's account.

Eager for the opportunity, Piest sprinted out of the pharmacy knocking on the truck window. Gacy rolled down his window and invited the kid for a ride. "Well, hell," John remembered saying. "Get in the truck. I gotta pick up something at my house. Then I got a meeting in Glenview. I'll drop you off on my way."

Piest got in the car, not about to waste an opportunity to make more money for his dream car. The way he described their conversation, Gacy insisted he couldn't hire a fifteen-year-old. Then Piest started to get antsy telling Gacy he was a hard worker and needed the money. Gacy began to twist the conversation. He brought up hustling. If Piest needed the cash, hustling would be a good fit, but Piest didn't take the bait.

At the house, the conversation continued about the job. They made their way to the rec room. Gacy offered him alcohol, but Piest refused. Soda would be fine. After a bit of talking, Piest spotted the handcuffs set out on the bar, and he asked Gacy what they were for. Gacy's handcuff trick came then, and the rest was lost, too. Darkness. Jack Hanley. The Other Guy. They were the ones with Piest.

9:30 came and went. Elizabeth Piest's son never came back inside. She ran out to the parking lot. Her son was gone as well as the contractor. Anxious, she drove home and told her husband about her son's disappearance.

Gacy woke from the darkness. Around ten, the phone rang. He was John again, coherent and aware. He answered. Richard Rapheal demanded to know why John had missed their meeting and where the hell John was. It was insulting to blow off an appointment. There were people waiting hours to speak with him. Rapheal later testified that Gacy had multiple excuses. A few included a flat tire, his uncle was dying, and he fell asleep.

Excuses accepted, John hung up the phone and returned to the bedroom. There he found Piest lying on the floor; the rope tied tightly around his neck. Piest's stiff body had wedged itself between the bed and the wall where it fell. Gacy struggled to pull his corpse out, careful to avoid the wet spot on the teenager's pants. He had urinated himself. Gacy showered, leaving

Robert's body on the bed, and headed to the hospital in hopes of seeing his uncle one last time. His uncle hadn't made it through the night. He arrived at the hospital too late, phoned his sister to tell her the news, and returned home to hide Piest in the attic.

Elizabeth Piest and her husband waited for their son at home until 11:30 pm, then they drove to the Des Plaines Police Station and filed a missing person report. Elizabeth brought with her the name of the contractor—John Wayne Gacy. They were told to wait until the morning, but waiting was the last thing on their mind.

The evening they thought they would spend with each other enjoying, laughing, and celebrating a family birthday quickly turned into one they could never forget. With the help of their older children, the Piests drove through the night in a desperate attempt to locate their son. The parents hopelessly toured Chicago's streets. Rob had seemingly vanished.

Tired and scared, the Piests returned to the station early the next morning. There had been no sign of their son. Detective James Pickall reached out to the Chicago police headquarters and asked for John Wayne Gacy's record. It was revealed then he'd been arrested several times and had a history of sodomy charges with underage boys. The police immediately knew he was violent and aggressive, and this time, there was no doubt Robert Piest was not a runaway. Lieutenant Kozenczak and three other officers made their way to 8213 Summerdale.

In a brown suit, Lieutenant Kozenczak knocked on Gacy's door. His demeanor calm and friendly, but he asked Gacy about a missing boy. The whole situation aggravated John. He relaxed, nonchalantly sitting in the living room recliner. He claimed he spoke to no one about a job opportunity, and he was busy arranging his uncle's funeral and had to call his mother. Lieutenant Kozenczak told him to call her now. Begrudgingly, Gacy called his mother and told her the news that Uncle Harold passed away while the police stood there. It pissed John off more. He told them he didn't have time to be questioned or to go down to the station. Lieutenant Kozenczak asked when he would. John replied, "Maybe in an hour. You guys are very rude. Don't you have any respect for the dead?"

With the promise of an hour, Lieutenant Kozenczak was satisfied. The officers left. Gacy hurried up to the attic, wrapping Piest's body in a blanket, and drove out to the bridge. When there was no one around, Gacy hauled the teenager's body out from the Oldsmobile's trunk and tossed him into the Des Plaines River. Piest's body floated down the very river he aspired to clean.

When Gacy finally arrived at the station, it was 3:12 in the morning on December 13th. It was a bitterly cold winter night. Unsettled and upset, Gacy was agitated, coming off a bit nervous. They informed him that Kozenczak had left around one.

Gacy came back to the station around noon. He spoke with Detective Pickall, making a written statement. He was sure to enlighten Pickall on how prominent he was in the community. He was a personal friend of the mayor as well as the First Lady, Rosalynn Carter. As Gacy talked on for hours, Kozenczak worked on getting a search warrant. And a little after three, Gacy was informed the police were going to be searching his home. He handed over his keys.

Under Surveillance

The Grexas watched, confused as the police arrived at Gacy's home. At 8213 Summerdale, they uncovered a variety of evidence, including the following: a copious number of pills, marijuana, pornographic films, handcuffs, and a two by four with holes drilled into it acting as some restraining device, fake police badges, dildos, an empty bottle with the stench of chloroform, and a starter pistol with blank shells. The following books were found hidden in the attic: *The American Bi-centennial Gay Guide; The Rights of Gay People, 21 Abnormal Sex Cases; The Great White Swallow; Heads & Tails; Bike Boy; Pederasty: Sex Between Men and Boys; Tight Teenagers.*

Lieutenant Kozenczak removed a photo receipt from Nisson Pharmacy in the kitchen trash, along with a thin rope. Shining a flashlight down into the crawl space revealed nothing. Robert Piest was not in the house.

With his cars impounded, Gacy left the police station on edge. Nothing official was charged, yet he knew it was only a matter of time. Upset, Gacy couldn't return to his home. The police put Gacy under twenty-four-hour surveillance on December 14th; so, he spent the night at his sister's.

More evidence was uncovered. They found bits of hair in the trunk of his car, its color matched Robert Piest's. Michael Rossi was brought in for questioning, but he had little intel. He just worked for Gacy. That was it. They spoke with Carole, who mentioned they might get information from his past employee John Butkovich. She mentioned how they were close. Finally, another lead that could expose John Wayne Gacy, but they quickly learned Butkovich had disappeared.

The more the investigators pieced everything together, the longer the list of past PDM employees who had gone missing grew. Rossi later mentioned a kid named Godzik who vanished. A high school class ring found in Gacy's dresser led them to the name John A. Szyc—another missing person as well. The case against Gacy grew, and the police hoped their suspect would crack under pressure. When Lillie Grexa asked her neighbor why he was being followed, he said the police were trying to link him to murder.

She asked about the victim—if it was his employees, the one that was missing. "Oh, no. Not him," Gacy said. "He's in another state." She inquired about a few other employees. It was the same answer. The charges revolving around drugs and substance misuse came up. He attempted to spin the whole thing. John Wayne Gacy made it clear to Lillie it was one massive misunderstanding. Every one of those employees could be accounted for with the excuse they left the state.

The pressure on Gacy mounted as the police trailed him. The days inched toward Christmas. His attitude was flippant and erratic. At bars, he'd order the investigators drinks and eat meals with them. Other times he asked them why he was being followed; they simply responded by telling him they were investigating a missing person.

On December 16th, it was six in the morning. The police had been tailing him the night before when Gacy was drunk, speeding around the city. The sun broke the horizon, and they stopped for breakfast at a diner. Any man would be exhausted, but Gacy appeared to have endless sources of energy. He asked them if they were sure they weren't feds working on a drug bust. That was the story Gacy wanted. "We're not with the feds," Officer Hachmeister said. "We're here because a kid is missing. Somebody must suspect that you know something about him."

"Hey, look, I talked to the kid only once. If he walked into this place now, I wouldn't even recognize him," Gacy said calmly. He went on telling them he was worried about the teenager as well. He played his role, made the officers think Gacy was a good guy. He had political connections and was friends with the First Lady, Rosalynn Carter.

All those political affiliations could not stop the steady stream of incriminating evidence being gathered. On December 18th, Mrs. Szyc provided the authorities with some of her son's papers. One of which was the warranty for a black and white Motorola TV. That very same model of Motorola had been found in Gacy's bedroom.

That night, Gacy invited Officers Schultz and Robinson over for dinner. Out of the officers following him, he had grown to trust these two in particular. It was around 6:30 in the evening when they arrived at 8213 Summerdale. Upon entering, they were hit with an awful smell. Gacy blamed it on his dog, soiling the newspaper in his kitchen. He let the dog out into the backyard and cleaned up the mess. He prepared perch and shrimp. As they ate, he gave them a tour of the house, showing them pictures of all the important people he knew, discussed his clown paintings, and discussed the plans for his second story addition to the rec room.

The visit seemed to be going smoothly. John Wayne Gacy might have felt as if he was making his case. The case that he was an ordinary guy with no reason to be suspected of these terrible accusations.

The night came to a grinding halt when Gacy let them know he had more work to take care of. There was a sudden shift in the atmosphere. The gracious host abruptly left his guests. He sped off, driving ninety miles an hour, doing his best to elude the police.

During this time, the serial number of the photo receipt found in Gacy's trash had been traced to Kim Byers. The log was dated December 11th. That bit of evidence became fairly damning because almost one week later, Kim told the police about how she absentmindedly slid the receipt into Rob's parka that night. That put Rob Piest at John Wayne Gacy's house the night he vanished.

December 19, the evidence continued to pour in. The tower of incriminating facts became overwhelming.

The two officers, Schultz and Robinson, stood outside in the nasty winter weather, waiting for Gacy to unlock the door. They noticed how his dog was tied up in the cold, icy rain.

"John, who left that dog out in this weather?" Schultz asked, scolding Gacy for the cruelty. John was unbothered by it. No one would be home to let it out; so, he tied it out back to a stake. Upon entering the home, they were hit once again with the harsh odor. Unlike the last time the two had visited, the dog hadn't been inside to have left a mess. Gacy moved them into the recreation room for drinks.

Unbeknownst to John Wayne Gacy, Schultz and Robinson had a plan to sneak into the suspect's bedroom and match the serial number of the Motorola TVs. If it were a match, they'd be able to place Szyc here as well. While Robinson distracted Gacy at the bar, Schultz made his way through the halls toward the back bathroom near the bedroom. He switched on the light and the exhaust fan, flushing the toilet in hopes of deafening out any sounds that would alert their host.

Using the flame of his cigarette lighter to see, Schultz moved quickly into the dark bedroom.

His heart may have been beating faster, his breath catching in his lungs. The officer swiftly located the serial number on the side of the TV. He repeated it silently several times to himself to help him remember the list of digits. All the while, Gacy stood a few feet on the other side of the wall.

Schultz returned to the bathroom and ran water in the sink. After flushing the toilet, a second time, hot air from the furnace turned on. Schultz froze. Here in the bathroom, the awful stench was worse as it blew up from the basement. Sour and nauseating. A scent Schultz knew but couldn't quite recall. His stomach sank. He returned to the recreation room, a sick feeling settling over.

The following day, Gacy's friendly demeanor toward his new buddies in law enforcement began to shift. Gacy's lawyer informed the police John was filing a $750,000 suit against the city of Des Plaines, Kozenczak, and several other officers. He claimed the surveillance was ruining his business and his civil rights were being violated.

Rossi and Cram were brought in for questioning.

David Cram told the police about digging beneath the house in the crawl space and spreading limestone. The officer handed Cram a paper and a pencil.

"Show me where you were digging."

Cram drew out a diagram. The young man explained, telling them Gacy had water issues, and that's why he was sent down into the cramped, dark space. They asked Cram for the dimensions. He figured they were about one to two feet wide—he held out his hands to give a rough estimate—and about two feet deep. The puzzle pieces began to align themselves. The officers asked what exactly was in the forbidden area. Cram described mounds of dirt about six feet in length and six inches high. The officers knew digging trenches that size made no sense, not for the work Gacy described. The realization came then—are the missing boys buried in the crawl space. They knew then that sitting there listening, something was buried beneath the floorboards of 8213, a secret Gacy did not want to be uncovered.

Officer Lang met with Schultz and Robinson after the interview with Cram. He recounted the details about the young employee digging in the crawl space. The discovery was now officially on record.

Later in the winter evening, as Schultz sat in his living room in front of the Christmas tree, the uneasy realization settled over him like a hard weight. Cook County Morgue. That was where he had met that pungent, putrid scent from Gacy's bathroom before. It was the stench of death.

Gacy visited with his lawyers around one o'clock in the morning on the twenty-first while the investigators hurried to draw up a warrant. John stayed in the offices speaking with his lawyers for what was supposed to be a quick fifteen minutes. Buried under stress, he took several Valium and drank heavily at the office, downing whatever was left in the Scotch bottle. Tears streaming from his eyes, Gacy confessed to killing over thirty people. Exhausted, he passed out on the couch of the office. The investigators waited patiently into the early hours of the morning. When the sun began to break over the gray winter sky, the lawyers came out. Although they couldn't divulge any information, they begged the police to arrest their client. Fear clearly shone in their eyes.

It was around eight in the morning when Gacy emerged. Gacy sped off to a Shell gas station his friend owned in a fog, hungover, and jumpy. He drove recklessly, speeding. The police close behind, shaken up by what the lawyers had told them. Officer Hachmeister jumped out of his car and started yelling at Gacy about driving like a "jag off." Instead of flying into a fit of rage, the word came over Gacy in one striking wave of defeat. Apologies poured from his mouth. His posture slumped.

The officers watched as Gacy attempted to slip three marijuana cigarettes into the pocket of a young gas station attendant. The attendant refused, but Gacy said, "Take it. The end is coming. These guys are going to kill me." His hope was to be arrested on a minor drug charge, but the police were hopeful the search warrant would be signed later that day. They'd wait.

Gacy drove to his friend Ron Rohde's house in Summerdale. They were reasonably good friends, but Gacy acted as though Rohde was his best friend. There, Gacy stayed for about half an hour in complete shambles. He babbled on about the end of his life, slurping down a morning scotch. Drunk and disorderly, he left. His head bobbed as he drove haphazardly, weaving between lanes. One of the officers became worried Gacy might attempt suicide by smashing into one of the bridge abutments.

Pulling up beside Gacy, the officers saw him clutching a rosary in his hand. The chase continued to David Cram's home. Michael Rossi stood outside in the driveway, unloading tools from a truck. Gacy begged Rossi to come inside the house. Reluctant at first, Rossi agreed. It didn't take long for the excuses to start pouring out. Inside Cram's home, tears streamed down his face. Gacy told the two how he confessed to the thirty murders. He referred to them as syndicate killings.

Gacy ended his round of goodbyes. Seeing Gacy was in no shape to get behind the wheel, Cram offered to drive. He had to meet with his lawyer LeRoy Stevens at a restaurant in the Northside to say goodbye. While Gacy stood beneath the canopy speaking to Stevens, Cram walked over to the officers. Gacy had one last destination. To go to the cemetery and visit his father's grave. "I'm really afraid the guy might try to kill himself and kill me with him. When we leave here, don't lose us, *please!*" Cram pleaded.

The pursuit continued.

Fear began to mount in the surveillance officers. They radioed into the station. They wanted to know if they should take Gacy down before taking his own life in one grand display before his father's tombstone. In his office, Kozenczak listened. The pressure was on. They couldn't lose Gacy. Not now.

Fifteen seconds passed.

"Yeah. Take him down," Kozenczak ordered.

December 21, 1979, the sun set high over the Chicago winter sky. It was around noon. They forced the car to a stop; then, five officers surrounded Gacy's car. Officer Robinson ripped open the passenger door; gun pointed at Gacy's right ear. "Get out of the car, John. You're under arrest."

As if his friends had betrayed him, Gacy asked in a weak tone, "What's the matter? What have I done?" Playing innocent didn't get him anywhere. He was immediately taken to the station, arrested on drug charges for placing marijuana in the gas attendant's pocket.

As Gacy was brought in for processing, Terry Sullivan finished up his work on the warrant and sent it to be signed by Judge Peters. The anxiety and fear pummeled Gacy. He had a heart attack there in the station. His chest became tighter and tighter. Gacy was rushed to the hospital only for doctors to find no sign of a heart attack. Simultaneously, the police were opening the doors of 8213 Summerdale.

The officers walked into the home, passed the plants and clown paintings to the bedroom; there, they opened the closet door, bent down, and pulled back the crawl space's trap door. The water rose above the ground, a murky black lake of death. They reconnected the sub pump and stood waiting as the water above the unmarked graves began to retreat.

When the water receded enough, Daniel Genty, evidence technician, dove deep into the crawl space's dwellings; on his hands and knees, he moved through the murky darkness. Right below the kitchen, a tuft of hair stuck out from beneath the soil. He shined his floodlight south and continued deeper where the ground was wet and spongy. Shining his light onto a puddle of reddish liquid, he witnessed hundreds of small, thin worms that scurried back into the mud after being exposed to the light. Genty carefully dug his entrenching tool into the ground. Spider webs and dust fell from the floorboards above where the other officers walked, waiting. The strong scent of sewage and waste continued permeating the air. Whitish material began to rise in the cloudy water. Genty knew what this was.

He immediately recognized the strange material. It was body tissue that had undergone chemical change after water exposure. He dug further down until his tool hit something hard. Human bone. It once belonged to someone's arm. Skin and hair barely clung to it.

"Charge him!" he shouted up to the officers gathered around the trap door, watching. His voice probably carried a bit of fear, anger, and adrenaline at the confirmation of the graveyard he uncovered.

"What?" Kozenczak hollered back.

"I've found one."

"What do you mean? You've found a body?"

"Yeah."

Genty returned to the trap door with a shovel full of the human remnants to show the other officers. "I think this crawl space is full of kids," he said. The weight of the contents he carried could not have been as heavy as the meaning behind his words.

Now out of the hospital and back at the station, Gacy received a prison uniform and was brought into a security room. A form was placed before him. A pen rested on the table. With trembling fingers, he signed a Miranda Rights waiver. He knew after meeting with the lawyers that it was over for him. After a few words, Gacy asked Officer Albrecht if he had been in the crawl space yet. The officer nodded.

"That's what the lime was for," Gacy said, his voice cold and empty.

Albrecht asked him what he meant.

"The lime was for the sewage dampness—and what you found there."

The questions came then, one after the other. And it didn't take much for Gacy to start confessing. In these first several interviews, Gacy was most honest. He began talking about Jack Hanley before his trial, building the case of insanity. It was around three in the morning, and Gacy decided he wanted to make a statement.

Over the next few days, he went into gruesome details. At times, the police struggled to listen, but they kept their composure. Hachmeister later described the confession. "He was having fun telling us about the murders in elaborate detail. He was trying to impress us. So, in my mind, if Gacy had more to tell—more victims out there or more bodies buried somewhere—he would have told us all about it."

News of the murders quickly reached the media. While he thrived from all the attention, John Wayne Gacy was upset by the press coverage. He'd been labeled as the "killer clown." He believed the press was twisting the truth.

In his mind, the injustice and mistreatment continued while he was incarcerated. In prison, he acted overly deserving and complained about his treatment. Gacy had great certainty that he would be acquitted and released. He continued to provide police with statements that included details of his sexual relations and the boys he killed. He saw them as lousy hustler types that wanted it.

February 6, 1980, was his first day of trial. Immediately his defense began to build the case that Gacy should be placed in a mental hospital, not a prison. It wasn't his fault. The Other Guy and Jack Hanley were all parts of his multiple personality disorder. But as the witnesses stepped forward and the evidence gathered held firm, it was clear that far too much planning and premeditation went into each kill for it to be the result of insanity.

The last witness stepped forward on Monday, March 10th. There had been over a hundred on the stand. The man was introduced as James Hanley, an officer who met Gacy at the bar Bruno's years ago. The one he embodied as he cruised Bug Square taking his victims. John Hanley had met Gacy once or twice before, but that was it.

When the court was adjourned, and both the prosecutors and defense rested their cases, Gacy strolled up to Ted Sullivan, the state attorney. In his hand, he waved a newspaper clipping with all the confidence he could muster.

"I'll see you at this party, Terry," Gacy chided. "And don't forget to bring my present. St. Patrick's Day, you know, is my birthday."

On March 12, Gacy was convicted guilty. At that time, he was charged with more murders than any other person in America. But Gacy appeared unnerved at the verdict. As he was led out of the courtroom, he winked at the deputy sheriff. As if the threat of the looming death sentence was no matter to him. And on the 13th, he was sentenced to death. Upon hearing the verdict, the courtroom erupted into a wave of applause. Most of which were the families who had lost precious members of their families.

He spent fourteen years in the Menard Correctional Center. There Gacy spent many hours in interviews with psychiatrists. He told them about his childhood and what little he could remember about the murders. He, himself, was curious of his motive. Gacy wanted to understand himself. He painted portraits of clowns hoping his art brought joy to people's lives and attempted to write a book so that others might hear his side.

He never won an appeal.

On May 9, 1994, Gacy was brought to the Stateville Correctional Center for execution after eating his last meal of fried chicken, French fries, Coke, and strawberry shortcake. He was pronounced dead at 12:58 am as the chemicals in lethal injection began coursing through his veins. His last words before slipping into a dark, empty unconsciousness— "Kiss my ass."

Bibliography

Amirante, Sam L. *John Wayne Gacy: Defending a Monster*. Skyhorse Publishing, 2015.

Cahill, Tim. *Buried Dreams: Inside the Mind of a Serial Killer*. Open Road Integrated Media; Open Road Media, 2014.

Crane, Tyler. *John Wayne Gacy: The True Crime Story of the Killer Clown*. EPUB, 2016.

Janos, Adam. "John Wayne Gacy's Childhood: 'Killer Clown' Serial Killer Was Victim of Abuse." A&E, September 15, 2020. https://www.aetv.com/real-crime/john-wayne-gacys-childhood.

John Wayne Gacy #237. Accessed February 10, 2021. http://www.clarkprosecutor.org/html/death/US/gacy237.htm.

"John Wayne Gacy." Biography.com. A&E Networks Television, October 21, 2020. https://www.biography.com/crime-figure/john-wayne-gacy.

"John Wayne Gacy." Crime Museum, July 19, 2017. https://www.crimemuseum.org/crime-library/serial-killers/john-wayne-gacy/.

Kissel, Ben, Marcus Parks, Henry Zebrowski, and Tom Neely. *The Last Book on the Left: Stories of Murder and Mayhem from History's Most Notorious Serial Killers*. Boston: Houghton Mifflin Harcourt, 2020.

Linedecker, Clifford L. *The Man Who Killed Boys*. New York: St. Martin's, 2003.

Rumore, Kori. "Timeline: Suburban Serial Killer John Wayne Gacy and the Efforts to Recover, Name His 33 Victims." chicagotribune.com. Chicago Tribune, June 21, 2019. https://www.chicagotribune.com/history/ct-john-wayne-gacy-timeline-htmlstory.html.

Sullivan, Terry, and Peter T. Maiken. *Killer Clown: The John Wayne Gacy Murders*. New York: Pinnacle Books, 2013.

Printed in Great Britain
by Amazon

53251777R00112